RELIGION
Gone Astray

What We Found *at the* Heart *of* Interfaith

Pastor Don Mackenzie, Rabbi Ted Falcon and Imam Jamal Rahman

Walking Together, Finding the Way®
SKYLIGHT PATHS®
PUBLISHING
Woodstock, Vermont

Religion Gone Astray:
What We Found at the Heart of Interfaith

2011 Quality Paperback Edition, First Printing
© 2011 by Don Mackenzie, Ted Falcon and Jamal Rahman

Library of Congress Cataloging-in-Publication Data
Mackenzie, Don, 1944–
Religion gone astray : what we found at the heart of interfaith / Don Mackenzie, Ted Falcon, and Jamal Rahman. — Quality paperback ed.
p. cm.
Includes bibliographical references.
ISBN 978-1-59473-317-8 (quality pbk. original) 1. Religions—Relations. 2. Abrahamic religions. I. Falcon, Ted. II. Rahman, Jamal. III. Title.
BL410.M33 2011
201'.5—dc23
2011032675

10 9 8 7 6 5 4 3 2 1

Manufactured in the United States of America
Cover design: Tim Holtz

SkyLight Paths is creating a place where people of different spiritual traditions come together for challenge and inspiration, a place where we can help each other understand the mystery that lies at the heart of our existence.

SkyLight Paths sees both believers and seekers as a community that increasingly transcends traditional boundaries of religion and denomination—people wanting to learn from each other, *walking together, finding the way.*

SkyLight Paths, "Walking Together, Finding the Way," and colophon are trademarks of LongHill Partners, Inc., registered in the U.S. Patent and Trademark Office.

Walking Together, Finding the Way®
Published by SkyLight Paths Publishing
A Division of LongHill Partners, Inc.
Sunset Farm Offices, Route 4, P.O. Box 237
Woodstock, VT 05091
Tel: (802) 457-4000 Fax: (802) 457-4004
www.skylightpaths.com

To the memory of M. K. Gandhi,
the Mahatma who continues to illuminate
the path to peace in a pluralistic world

Contents

Preface

At the conclusion of most of our presentations, we sing our theme song. The words to that song are in Arabic, Hebrew, and English. When we introduce the song, Imam Jamal shares the Arabic and then translates, Rabbi Ted does the same with the Hebrew, and then Pastor Don gives the English, "It's all one, and I AM as I AM." Usually he simply repeats the English by way of "translation." But at one of our presentations, something totally incomprehensible came out of his mouth instead of the repeated English. Rabbi Ted remembers it contained phrases like, *"Je ne c'est quoi,"* and "All that Hoo-Hah." It was so unexpected that Rabbi Ted and Imam Jamal burst out laughing.

Not all of our presentations bring such hilarity, but we almost always learn something new from our interactions with groups across the country. It has become somewhat standard for one of us to say, when we are inviting questions, "We have some time for questions now. We don't have any time for answers, but we welcome your questions!"

The truth is that this book is one consequence of the questions we have been asked at the many speaking engagements we have had since the publication of our first book, *Getting to the Heart of Interfaith: The Eye-Opening, Hope-Filled Friendship of a Pastor, a Rabbi and a Sheikh* (SkyLight Paths), two years ago. We talk about the core teachings of our faiths, and we share aspects of our traditions that are aligned with those teachings. Then we share problematic texts that seem contrary to the core teachings of our own faiths. And this is when the questions really begin to flow.

At just about every presentation we've given, we have been asked, "How can we talk with those who think they have the only truth?" It seems that more people than ever are finally asking these questions: How can we talk to each other? What is it that separates us and makes cooperation so difficult? Can't we get beyond it?

We also hear this: What about the violence done in the name of religion? We have met many people who either condemn religion because of the violence done in its name, or who have left their faith because of that awareness. Why is violence associated with religion? Is there anything we can do about that?

Another recurring question focuses on sexism: How can we deal with the outdated patriarchal system in religion? From women, we often get questions about the inequality of men and women in religious institutions. What are we to do with texts that condemn women to subservient roles?

Finally, we are often asked Why religion is so antagonistic toward gay and lesbian people. We've had questions raised by those in the GLBT (gay, lesbian, bisexual, transgendered) community and those concerned about them. Why is religion so antagonistic toward alternative sexual practices? Why isn't love the criterion for acceptable relationships? The whole society is beginning to accept gays and lesbians. Why can't religion be inclusive?

These four issues are raised again and again, reflecting the pain that many experience as a result of prohibitions, inhibitions, and exclusivities of religious institutions. There is the personal pain when we are victims of these issues or when actions in the name of faith are clearly in conflict with the spiritual teachings we hold dear; communal pain when rifts form within faith communities over the legitimacy of these issues and our reactions to them; and interreligious pain when faith traditions condemn other traditions for the evil that exists in the world.

The exclusivity, violence, inequality of men and women, and homophobia that have been attributed to our texts and have caused deep personal, communal and interreligious pain throughout the world comprise the focus of this book. Because our understanding of God and revelation informs all our thinking, we include those topics following our discussion of these four problem areas. We will also consider the possibility that these problematic texts can contribute to our cooperation and healing as a society, rather than to our alienation, our going astray, from our spiritual identity.

In these four major areas, religions go astray from their own core teachings. But those very core teachings can provide support for the healing that is sorely needed, and can call us back to our spiritual purpose.

When Moses came down from Mount Sinai, he discovered that the people had lost heart, had gone astray. They had regressed into idolatry. What happened next? Moses called them back.

When the disciples, at a loss for what to do next, went fishing after the crucifixion, Jesus appeared to them on the shore of the Sea of Tiberius and called them back.

And to the seventh-century pagans, and to those Jews and Christians who strayed from monotheism in the Arabian Peninsula, the Prophet Muhammad proclaimed, "There is no god but God." He called them back.

Religions come into being to call us back to the spiritual paths from which we have strayed, the paths that lead to healing. But religions themselves, as institutions, go astray, too. Losing sight of their greater purpose, they serve themselves. We might recognize the pain when we lose sight of our own personal purpose, yet our religious institutions seem less able to acknowledge when they have strayed from their purpose. Like us, religious institutions need to be called back.

We believe that interfaith dialogue holds the key to a healing that calls us back to purpose and to meaning. In the ten years that we have been working closely with each other, we have risked confronting aspects of our traditions usually hidden, and the consequences have been deeply life-affirming. We risk becoming vulnerable as we share awkward and even unacceptable texts and interpretations, but it is this very vulnerability that allows our dialogue to move forward.

The healing that we need as a society requires us to meet each other as full human beings. The healing we seek opens us up to collaborate more honestly in confronting the major issues that impact us all. Such healing does not deny the problems we find in our traditions, but utilizes them in the service of becoming whole. Healing allows us to appreciate our own traditions and those of others more profoundly.

We call this process the "escalation of hope." Our journey is a serious one, but it invites deeper friendship and even laughter. We invite you to join us as we set the stage to discuss some of the most difficult issues that face our three faiths and search for ways to heal the significant rifts those issues have created among them.

Introduction

What We Found at the Heart of Interfaith

Sam Harris began the work on his book *The End of Faith* right after the horrible events of September 11, 2001. *The End of Faith* focuses on the violent aspects of the Abrahamic religions, and particularly on the violence of radical Islam. His answer, like the answers of many whose writing was inspired by that day of destruction, is that religion itself is the enemy. He does not believe that peaceful coexistence is possible because of the inherently war-like influences of Judaism, Christianity, and Islam.

Our work together also began in earnest immediately following the events of 9/11. But we drew very different conclusions. We have learned that we need to acknowledge the violent tendencies in our religions, but we also need to acknowledge the deep spiritual teachings that flow from these very traditions. To advocate the dissolution of our faiths can only lead to greater animosity and suspicion. This is not the path of dialogue toward greater understanding. We believe that the realities of 9/11 call for all of us to delve more deeply into the institutional basis for the allegations that Sam Harris and others have made.

At one of our presentations, a participant challenged us: Wouldn't the world be a far more peaceful place without the religious institutions that battle each other? We agreed that our institutions tend to view their own adherents as far more worthy than others. But we also recognize that these institutions provide a necessary framework for spiritual awareness. Spirituality might be seen as the water of life, but without a glass, it is far more difficult to drink. At best, the institution serves as the container. At worst, the institution believes it alone has access to the water and is unaware when the container, in fact, is empty.

We strive not to destroy our religious traditions but to understand and appreciate them more deeply. To do so, not only must we be willing to recognize the great spiritual teachings of each religion, but also the ways in which each of our traditions has strayed from them. We seek to honor the gifts as well as the challenges of our Abrahamic faiths because we believe that this is the path toward greater hope and greater healing.

The excruciating explosions of 9/11 shattered our sense of safety and stunningly revealed the gaps in our interfaith awareness. Our virtual ignorance of Islam contributed to the ease with which the media could demonize Muslims and portray them all as terrorists. The 9/11 attacks awakened us to the need for more effective interfaith dialogue.

We have spent more time with each other since 9/11 than we ever could have imagined. When the three of us started working together, we barely knew one another. Looking back, it is striking to see how much we have changed.

During the years we have worked together, we have learned that true interfaith dialogue cannot focus solely on sharing the sweetness of each tradition. We must also become more honest with each other as we share those aspects of our traditions with which we are less than comfortable. We become more vulnerable as we share our discomforts, and our vulnerability enables our relationships to grow deeper.

Our Experience as "The Other"

At one of our many meals together—this particular time at a Seattle bar and grill—our server looked at the three of us and said, "So is this the beginning of a joke—'A rabbi, a pastor, and an imam walk into a bar ... '?'" We came up with our own punch line: "They ordered two martinis and a root beer!" But sometimes the attention we draw is more serious in nature.

Following our presentations, we often feel euphoria and exhaustion and hope to find a quiet place to unwind together. After an event in the Northeast, we went back to our hotel, where the bar, in the far corner area of the large hotel lobby, was still open. We headed for cushioned chairs around a low round table, a little parade—Rabbi Ted in his *kippah,* Pastor Don in his clerical collar, and Imam Jamal in his signature collarless shirt—each of us carrying the scriptures we had used during our presentation. As we passed the only other occupied table, Ted and Jamal were uncomfortably aware of the unfriendly glances of the four young and somewhat inebriated men sitting there. "What have we here?" they muttered, "A rabbi ... a Muslim ... and will ya' look at that—it's a minister, collar and all. What's a Christian doing with *them*?" They sneered at the three of us over their shoulders.

Neither Ted nor Jamal said anything about this at first, but both were on alert for trouble. Don neither saw nor heard what Ted and Jamal couldn't help but notice—that this was not a safe place for them; that aggression could be directed at them at any moment.

A straight, white, male Protestant minister would have less cause to fear anything, but for Ted and Jamal, this was not the case.

Many Jews of Ted's generation grew up with invisible antennae, always on guard for threatening environments. He feels most comfortable in New York and Los Angeles because, while Jews are still not in the majority there, these are cities with substantial Jewish populations and a living awareness of Jewish culture. But even in those places, there is an unconscious vigilance that never quite goes away. This is something that is often difficult for non-Jews to understand, unless they, too, have lived as a distinct minority, and have a personal and group history of persecution. It's like trying to tell someone who has never experienced a panic attack what it's like to have one. He or she may understand it intellectually, but it is impossible to "get it" on a visceral level.

Because Jamal's parents were diplomats and moved every two years, he grew up living in many countries where he was among the majority culture; as a result, he did not develop this deeply ingrained awareness of otherness. Unless Jews live in Israel, this is not an experience that they ever have (and even there, they are surrounded by hostile neighbors). But since 9/11, Imam Jamal has perceived his minority status as a Muslim in America in a new way. Overnight, his personal safety became threatened in a way it had not previously been. He got pulled out of airplane security lines for extra scrutiny. He knew that there were certain places he probably shouldn't go, and a nearly empty bar with four young guys who'd had too much to drink was probably among them.

We ordered our drinks (two martinis and a root beer) and a light snack and chatted about the evening's program and how it had gone. Don relaxed into his chair but Ted and Jamal, while appearing to be unaware of the continuing taunts behind them, remained vigilant.

Finally, Ted said, "Are you guys aware of the energy coming at us from that table?"

Jamal nodded. "Yes," he said. "I've been aware of them since we came in. They started making remarks about us right away."

Don looked concerned, as he realized that he had not made the same observations.

We didn't look at them because we knew that would have been provocative, but, even so, we could hear that one of the guys was more outspoken than the others. It was as if he was inciting them, trying to whip them up into something that would explode in the room. But there was another voice, too, one that in its good-humored tone, we could tell was working on defusing the situation.

Without discussing it, we all knew that what we had to do was what we always did: share our prayers before we ate and drank. We were not about to hide. Ted went first, repeating the traditional words in Hebrew. Then Don, saying grace, and Jamal giving thanks for the food in Arabic.

We became so focused on the blessing of the moment that it was as if our energy was withdrawn from the room. While this was happening, the four guys at the other table got up and left. First we were aware of the quiet, and then we turned to see an empty table across the bar.

Strangely enough, it was Pastor Don who seemed most shaken by this incident. Experiencing the animosity with which Ted and Jamal are deeply familiar gave him the visceral realization that he, too, could be an object of hatred, that people could be dangerously angry at him, just for being with Ted and Jamal.

For Rabbi Ted and Imam Jamal, it was another in a long line of situations in which they had felt concern simply for being who they are. For Pastor Don, it was another door opening into the experience of being the other. For all of us, it underscored the importance of our work in support of peaceful relations among faiths, and it illustrated the difference between being a member of a majority tradition and being a member of a minority tradition.

The sight of three religious leaders from three different traditions walking together should be a welcome sight. Until it is universally so, we still have work to be done.

The Stages of Interfaith Dialogue

Early on in our work together, we realized that we were creating a way to help ourselves and others become more intentional and conscious of how interfaith dialogue can happen. We identified five stages of interfaith dialogue that can help us all experience the many possibilities for healing that interfaith dialogue and collaboration can provide. They are:

Stage 1: Sharing stories to move beyond separation and fear

Stage 2: Appreciating our core teachings

Stage 3: In the context of our core teachings, sharing consistencies and inconsistencies

Stage 4: Engaging in more difficult conversations

Stage 5: Experiencing spiritual practices from other traditions

As you read through these stages, you can see how one naturally leads to the next. In our own relationship, stage 1 consisted of simply talking to each other and sharing stories and aspects of our traditions that have influenced the directions of our spiritual paths. This sharing naturally led to appreciating the core teachings of each of our traditions (stage 2). Next, we began to share some of the texts and beliefs that flowed from and supported our core teachings, along with our realization that there are parts of our traditions inconsistent with our own core teachings. Naming these inconsistent verses and beliefs in each of our traditions opened the way for much more honest sharing (stage 3). At first we labeled those aspects awkward. Later, we realized that some of them—such as exclusivity, violence, inequality of men and women, and homophobia—are simply unacceptable.

Because we had spent time becoming more vulnerable by sharing troubling aspects of our traditions, we were ready to share some of the more difficult conversations (stage 4). One of these continuing topics has to do with the Middle East. Although we each support full human rights for both Israelis and Palestinians, we clearly have different points of view. We do not always agree, and sometimes our disagreements are vigorous. But we strive to keep our hearts open as we engage in this challenging step in the process of interfaith dialogue.

Finally, we reach that place where we can dispel the fear that interfaith dialogue will weaken our own faith and rob us of our identity. We celebrate the spiritual dimensions of another faith (stage 5). The differences between and among our faiths can focus our awareness of the universals to which they each point. The understanding of our differences can, finally, help us each to grow spiritually.

But, it turns out that there is far more to that third stage than we had realized. In this book, we go much more deeply into the particular texts and beliefs that are inconsistent with our core teachings. But what are these core teachings? In what ways are each of our faiths consistent with the teachings that are at their heart? And in what ways do they betray them?

Core Teachings of the Abrahamic Traditions

While at their centers, all of our traditions include the same universal teachings, history and culture conspired for each to have a particular emphasis.

Oneness is the core teaching of Judaism. Where once this One was represented by a single heavenly being, the awareness of One has evolved to embrace an absolutely inclusive oneness. Everything is interconnected, and we are all a part of the One. This core teaching is expressed in the *Sh'ma*, the central tenet of Jewish faith: "Listen, Israel, the Eternal One (Absolute Inclusive Being) is our God (the One Life awakening within each of us), the Eternal is One" (Deuteronomy 6:4; author's translation). These words infuse all of Jewish spiritual teaching; they constitute the essential core of Jewish tradition.

Unconditional love is the core teaching of Christianity. Loving unconditionally means that there is nothing you can do to make me stop loving you. My love for you is not dependent on any condition. This is what Jesus meant when he said, "But I say to you, love your enemies and pray for those who persecute you" (Matthew 5:44). It is also what he intended when he said toward the end of his ministry, "This is my commandment, that you love one another as I have loved you" (John 15:12).

Compassion is the core teaching of Islam. All but one of the 114 chapters of the Qur'an begin with the words, *"Bismillah ir Rahman ir Rahim—*In the name of God, boundlessly compassionate, infinitely merciful." Compassion is the essence of God and defines God's message to humanity. The greatest provision for our journey of life is the understanding and practice of compassion for self and for others.

Our core teachings provide a standard of measurement, a way of discerning the consistent and inconsistent verses and beliefs of each of our traditions.

Some Particulars Consistent with Our Core Teachings

Each of our faiths has rituals, practices, and insights that support these core teachings. Here are examples from each of our traditions.

JUDAISM'S WEEKLY REMINDER OF MEANING AND PURPOSE

Shabbat, the Sabbath, is a particular observance in Judaism that helps us walk the core teaching of Oneness into the world. Shabbat marked the completion and the fulfillment of the biblical story of creation and reminds us that creation has meaning and purpose.

Each week of our lives is a week of creation, and Shabbat offers us the opportunity to conclude each week with blessing. It invites us to release the need for things to be any other than they are. It is a weekly reminder of a peaceful state of consciousness that can awaken at any time. In those precious moments, our perception of separateness and fragmentation dissolve, and we celebrate the wonder of the life we share. The consciousness of Shabbat brings with it reminders of the meaning and purpose of our lives and the preciousness of our connection to all that is.

CHRISTIANITY'S AWAKENING TO FORGIVENESS AND RENEWAL

The resurrection of Jesus is a faith conviction from Christianity that awakens us to unconditional love. For many, this story is taken literally and nourishes a personal relationship to the messianic character of Jesus. But stopping at the literal meaning neglects the deeper meaning of the story. The literal particulars of the story, that Jesus came back to life on the first day of the week, serve to communicate that God can always make everything new. God always forgives us. God always gives us another chance. It is never too late. This is the power of unconditional love.

ISLAM'S SPIRITUALITY OF MIND AND HEART

Ilm (knowledge) is a great teaching of Islam, leading us to a deeper practice of compassion. *Ilm*, the second most frequently used word in the Qur'an after *Allah* (the Arabic word for God), points to a holistic way of understanding. It combines the functions of the mind and heart. The Prophet Muhammad teaches us to move from the knowledge of the tongue to the knowledge of the heart because "the heart in no way falsified" what it sees (53:11). By expanding our heart knowledge, we move into that space where true compassion, empathy, and forgiveness are possible. In Islam, we identify *ilm* as a great blessing.

Examples of Particulars Inconsistent with Our Core Teachings

Just as we have practices within our traditions that can be identified as consistent with our faith's core teachings, so, too, we have practices that are inconsistent with them. These inconsistencies are all examples of religion gone astray. We will be exploring these at greater length but want to give you an idea of what fits in this category.

Rabbi Ted says that if a Jew imagines that Jews are the only chosen people, this is inconsistent with the reality of Oneness. Pastor Don says that when Christians say that Christianity is the only way to God, that is inconsistent with the unconditional love that is central to the Gospel of Jesus. And Imam Jamal says that if a Muslim claims that the Qur'an is superior to the Torah and the Christian Scriptures,* this is inconsistent with the inclusivity of compassion.

So Who Are We?

Part of the problem is that as individuals and as institutions, we have both a separate self and the greater self. When we are identified only by what we do and what we have, we experience our separate self,

---

*While we have used the phrase "Christian Scriptures" in place of the more usual "New Testament" because of the supersessionist nature of the latter, it should be noted that for Pastor Don and many others, "Christian Scriptures" includes not only the specifically Christian material but also the Jewish biblical texts. In this book, we mean this term to point specifically to the Christian literature usually called the New Testament.

and when we transcend those outer definitions of self and awaken to the deeper nature of our being, we experience our greater self. Spiritual practices help us awaken to our greater self. The better able we are to discern which identity we experience in each moment, the better able we are to avoid unnecessary pain and anguish in our lives.

As individuals, we stray from our spiritual identity in myriad ways. Although we aspire to become better human beings and to contribute to the common good, we get caught up in the drama of daily life and lose sight of these priorities. We fall prey to such human inclinations as greed and selfishness. We focus on our individual needs alone and neglect our commitment to evolve into the fullness of our being and to serve others as well as ourselves.

Our institutions go astray when, like the separate self, they forget the essential nature of their being. We call the aspects of our traditions that are inconsistent with our core teachings manifestations of their "shadow side." They are often defensive reactions to perceptions of threats from the outside.

While we may be willing to admit the shadow side of our separate selves, the part that longs for power and control, it is more difficult to acknowledge that side in the spiritual communities that we create. But it is we who have created our religious institutions, and they bear our imprint for good and for ill. When feeling threatened, they respond with defensiveness, anger, even aggression. How else can we understand the kind of violence that has issued from religious establishments over the centuries? Still, we tend to defend our institutions no matter how far they have gone astray.

The Beginning of Healing

We believe that naming the issues we share is the beginning of the healing process by which our separate, individual identity and our greater, more universal self become better integrated. We will do that in the following chapters as directly as possible, looking at context and commentary when that is helpful, and identifying the activities of our shadow-self on individual as well as institutional levels. And we will talk about some responses to these continuing issues that can be healing for us all. We will cast an appreciative light on the clarity and the relevance of the deep core teachings of each of our faiths. There is a great deal of healing to be found within our own traditions.

Toward Greater Healing and Hope

Our willingness to explore uncomfortable aspects of our traditions is part and parcel of the hope we experience. We invite you to consider your own truths as you read these pages. We affirm that sharing our differences can provide the most stable support and inspiration for dialogue. As you read our views on God and revelation, we encourage you to explore how your own beliefs can support greater healing and wholeness.

So, welcome to the deeper dimensions of interfaith dialogue. This book is not intended to be a comprehensive look at any one issue. Rather, it is a highly personal exploration informed by personal experience—our work together—and the generous feedback received from the people with whom we interact. We hope that many of the topics in this book can form the focus for discussion groups within your own community and between your community and others.

Let us together learn how to share our truths, celebrate our differences, and work together on the kind of collaboration that can bring healing to us all.

Some Suggestions on How to Use This Book

Our comments on exclusivity, violence, the inequality of men and women, and homophobia form the central four chapters of this book. These are the specific areas where we see that our religious institutions have gone astray and have drifted from their essential spiritual purpose. This is a new way of looking at these aspects of our traditions, so you will find additional material at the end of each of these chapters to help deepen your understanding.

Sharing Our Stories

We include stories from our adventures together over the years that we have worked together. Because much of the material we share has sprung from our presentations, we hope that you can get some of the flavor of that process. Stories communicate in special ways, and we hope that our own stories help you appreciate your own journey.

Questions for Discussion

The questions we have included following each of the four main chapters are not meant as a test—they are meant to stimulate your own thinking about the issues raised. Although you will find it helpful to think about them on your own, they are particularly suitable for discussion with another person or sharing in a group. We hope that our words provide a foundation on which you can build your own nourishing and enlightening discussions. Sharing our truths provides a doorway to expanding meaningful and healing communication and then prompting action to better the world.

Spiritual Practices

You will notice throughout this book that our own spiritual practices are essential in our lives. We strongly urge you to explore the spiritual practices in your own faith tradition and to deepen the ones to which you are already committed. We provide meditation exercises from each of our traditions that are specific to the particular chapters they follow. We believe that such practices can help us all reclaim the essential spiritual wisdom we already carry within ourselves. We all have spiritual awareness available to us as our birthright, and meditative practice provides support for awakening consciously to our deeper being. We suggest that you experiment with one of the verses or phrases we provide in each section as a focus for meditation.

Repeat the phrase you choose until you have it committed to memory, and then close your eyes and repeat it silently and slowly. Let it serve as the focus for moments of silence. We strongly suggest that you keep a meditation journal to record your experience each time you meditate on one of these verses. We have found that this allows us to witness the rhythms of our meditations in clearer ways and to learn from our experiences.

Our Sources

Rabbi Ted's biblical quotations are taken from the *JPS Hebrew-English TANAKH* (Philadelphia: Jewish Publication Society, 2000) unless otherwise indicated.

Pastor Don's biblical quotations are taken from the *New Revised Standard Version Bible* (New York: Division of Christian Education of the National Council of the Churches of Christ in the United States of America, 1989).

Imam Jamal's Qur'anic translations are primarily from Yusuf Ali, *The Meaning of the Holy Qur'an* (Beltsville, MD: Amana Publications, 1989). Other translations used are Muhammad Asad, *The Message of the Qur'an* (Bath, UK: The Book Foundation, 2003), and Camille Helminski, *The Light of Dawn: Daily Readings from the Holy Qur'an* (Boston: Shambhala, 2000).

We Are the Healing That Needs to Be

This book is dedicated to Mahatma Gandhi, the Indian philosopher and activist famous for his teachings on nonviolent resistance to oppression and his lifelong commitment to social change through nonviolent means. When he taught, "Be the change you want to see in the world," he empowered us all to participate in the inner and the outer healing that needs to be. We hope this book will contribute to a more effective dialogue among religious and nonreligious people and groups who sincerely care about issues of social justice and earth care. We look forward to the time when all of us join together to be the healing that needs to be.

Chapter One

Exclusivity

Staking Claim to a One and Only Truth

When our tradition is grounded in the belief that ours is superior to others', we often have the basis for serious discord. If my faith is the only way to God and to Heaven, and the only way to avoid hell, then I cannot help making negative judgments about those who do not accept my faith. Such feelings of exclusivity can even lead to violence in the name of our own understanding of faith and of God. In fact, exclusivity is often at the heart of all issues of our traditions that are inconsistent with their core teachings.

Exclusivity in Judaism
Personal Reflections

Our personal stories are an essential part of our interfaith journey. The examination of our πearly conditioning can shed light on the source of many of the issues that we face today. Exploring my early conditioning held some surprises for me. In retrospect, the warm and accepting home in which I grew up may not have been so warm and accepting after all.

I learned about my religious identity as much by what we did not do as by what we did. I learned that I am Jewish but not Orthodox. My family did not follow traditional laws of kashrut (keeping kosher), when we prayed my father and I did not wear yarmulkes (the skullcaps worn by traditional Jews), and our prayer books included both English and Hebrew.

We were Reform Jews, celebrating Shabbat before dinner on Friday nights with blessings over candles, wine, and bread. Unlike more traditional Jews, we drove on Shabbat, and often attended Friday evening services. The impression I got was that we were far more modern in our observance than our traditional counterparts. Contrary to the opinion of more traditional family members, we thought ours was clearly a more enlightened version of Judaism.

My mother was the reader in the household, and virtually all the books that earned a place on the shelves at home had Jewish content. More specifically, most of these books focused on Israel and on the pursuit of social justice as a Jewish value. Reform Judaism, particularly in those days, concentrated on the prophetic message of social justice far more than on ritual observance. But Friday nights were for family. It was not until my last years in high school that I ever went anywhere other than home or temple on that night.

I learned that we were a minority, and we had to work for the rights of other minorities. We supported equal rights for African-Americans and celebrated the fact that a Jew, Kivie Kaplan, was an early head of the NAACP. But black people were not our neighbors. Our neighbors were white Christians.

It was crucial that we preserve Jewish identity, particularly in the midst of a majority culture that did not seem to think highly of Judaism. Keeping ourselves separate, particularly with respect to Jews only marrying other Jews, was taught as a key to our survival as a people. I still remember the intense discomfort I felt the first—and only—time I danced with a non-Jewish girl in high school.

I was captivated by her beautiful blue eyes, and finally got up the nerve at a school party to ask her to dance with me. She was as tall as I was, with very dark hair and very light skin. Suddenly, I lost the power of speech. Forbidden! Dangerous! The voices of sharp recrimination within me seemed to burn through every cell in my body. I could barely finish the dance. I can't imagine what she thought, but it would be almost twenty years before I tried that again. I don't think I ever told my parents about it.

Although I did have non-Jewish friends, I only went to church a few times, when my family attended weddings or funerals. At those times, I received very strict instructions: We do not kneel. We do not go forward for communion. When singing Christmas songs in school, I was to mouth the word *Christ* when others sang it. We were different, and that difference needed to be maintained. Jews were not to have Christmas trees or celebrate that wintertime holiday.

Most people around us believed that a man named Jesus was the Son of God who came to save all people. I was taught that we do not believe that. But it got more complicated because Christians seemed to believe that we Jews killed Jesus. I didn't understand how someone could kill the Son of God but learned that this was not something to talk about with non-Jews.

In my father's family, Christians were called *goyim*, literally "nations," but referring specifically to Christians. It was a compliment to be told by my paternal grandfather that I had a *yiddishe kop*, a Yiddish phrase meaning a "Jewish head," and signifying intelligence. *Goyishe kop*, or "non-Jewish head," referred to someone who lacked such intelligence, namely, some non-Jews. I learned later that this was symptomatic of the ways a minority asserts its superiority in the midst of many signs of its powerlessness.

To be honest, I found it difficult to understand how the Christians could believe as they did. They seemed to have a kind of certainty of belief that I did not experience. In my Reform Jewish upbringing, I was not taught that God wrote the Torah, or that Torah represented the exact words God spoke to Moses. There were passages that made sense to me and passages that did not. But I learned there was deep meaning in the call of the prophets to social justice, and in the striking ethical clarity of some Torah verses.

I was not asked to believe anything like my perception of the Christian faith story. The only other religion I interacted with in those days was Christianity, and though, along with many Jews, I envied the energy surrounding Christmas, I could not understand how the vast majority of people could subscribe to the story of the crucified and resurrected Savior. The world did not look to me like a Savior had come. Wasn't the Messiah supposed to bring peace and love among all people? War, racism, and anti-Semitism seemed like ample evidence that the Messiah had not yet arrived.

As I look back, I realize that I was conditioned to believe that our religion was better than the majority religion of our culture, that the Christian culture around us lacked a certain kind of coherence. Religion, though it was often a major topic of concern at home, was not something to be discussed with non-Jewish friends.

I learned that the Christians held the power. Jews were a minority and were often treated badly by those in power. I was born during the Holocaust and learned that a Jew could not fully trust the Christian community. There was always the possibility that we could find ourselves alone against the accusations of the majority culture. Only Israel, achieving Jewish statehood when I was six years old, stood as a guarantor of Jewish survival. If all else failed, we Jews could always go there to live.

Judaism, as we understood it, was a religion of reason that welcomed the teachings of science. We believed in evolution, understanding that the creation myths of the Torah reflected ancient attempts to understand how everything came to be. As an adolescent, I no longer believed that God was an Old Man Up There, and I learned that questions about the nature of God were welcome in Judaism. The only creed I was asked to recite contained the assertion that God is One.

The Judaism of my childhood seemed flexible. It allowed various opinions, and it welcomed scientific views of the world. I was taught that this was not true of Christianity, which was inflexible, demanded adherence to particular beliefs, and often fought the discoveries of science. If a Christian friend did not fit this picture, I assumed that he was "less Christian" than others. Although my parents considered our home to be a prejudice-free zone, that pertained to our feelings regarding African-Americans, not Christians. We did not hold Christianity in high regard. It was always something of a mystery to me why so many people were Christian and so few people were Jewish.

Of course, I learned later that my early beliefs were flawed. In college, I found Christian thinkers like Paul Tillich and Reinhold Niebuhr revealing a Christianity of far greater depth. Nevertheless, the separation persisted. Only two fraternities on campus admitted Jews, and often the fall semester began on one of the Jewish High Holy Days.

Bridging the distance, and increasing our knowledge and appreciation of each other's traditions have become part of my life's work. So it is necessary for me to acknowledge not only my personal conditioning, but also aspects of Judaism that reinforce misunderstandings and distance.

Scriptural and Institutional Support for Exclusivity

In our conversations and in our teaching, it is common for Pastor Don and Imam Jamal to comment on the ways in which their scriptures refer to Jews and to Judaism. I often feel at a loss during those particular conversations. As the earliest of the three Abrahamic faiths, there is obviously no mention of Christianity or Islam in the Torah or in the entire *Tanach*, the Hebrew Bible. The essential claims to exclusivity that are made in Jewish Scripture occur prior to either of those other religions, in the context of earlier expressions of pagan faith. Judaism proclaimed the Oneness of God and saw itself as unique in bringing that crucial message. The belief in One began the awareness that would evolve into an appreciation that all people are united by that One, and then to the realization that we are all part of that One.

The Torah, which is the most sacred of Jewish biblical texts, puts the matter quite plainly:

> I will maintain My covenant between Me and you, and your offspring to come, as an everlasting covenant throughout the ages, to be God to you and to your offspring to come.
>
> *(Genesis 17:7)*

> For you are a people consecrated to the LORD your God: the LORD your God chose you from among all other peoples on earth to be His treasured people.
>
> *(Deuteronomy 14:2)*

Being chosen comes with responsibilities, for the children of Israel were obligated to follow the requirements of that covenant. Some of those actions were proper ritual observance and some were proper ethical behavior:

> Now then, if you will obey Me faithfully and keep My covenant, you shall be My treasured possession among all the peoples.
>
> *(Exodus 19:5)*

Furthermore, the people themselves also have priestly responsibilities, because there is something holy about their nature. While the actual priesthood remained the province of the descendents of Aaron, the first high priest, each member of the community possesses a unique holiness:

> Indeed, all the earth is Mine, but you shall be to Me a kingdom of priests and a holy nation.
>
> *(Exodus 19:6)*

At the core of this concept is the belief in the special covenant between God and the people Israel:

> It is not because you are the most numerous of peoples that the LORD set His heart on you and chose you—indeed, you

are the smallest of peoples; but it was because the LORD favored you and kept the oath He made to your fathers....

(Deuteronomy 7:7–8)

Because the Hebrew people were chosen for the way of One, they had responsibilities that other peoples did not. The one God demanded ethical behavior, since those who knew the spiritual nature of creation had responsibility to care for that creation. Human beings were seen as God's messengers on earth. And, as the understanding of the implications of oneness evolved, it became clearer that we are all sharing One Life. Because this is so, it is necessary to treat others as you would wish to be treated yourself. It is from this awareness of One that what we call the golden rule evolved in virtually all spiritual traditions. Since each of us is an expression of a shared God, how we treat others is essentially how we are treating ourselves.

Contrary to this teaching of oneness, of course, is the claim that Jews and the Jewish way are superior to others. In some of the mystical texts, the Jewish soul is seen as purer than that of non-Jews, but later commentators understand such statements to refer to pagans, those who are not able to appreciate oneness.

Commentary on Exclusivity

Most current responses to the idea that Jews are the "chosen" people include the belief that all peoples are chosen for their unique way. In a widely published statement, Rabbi Lord Immanuel Jakobovits, a former Modern Orthodox chief rabbi of England, reflects this point of view clearly:

> Yes, I do believe the chosen people concept as affirmed by Judaism in its holy writ, its prayers, and its millennial tradition. In fact, I believe that every people—and indeed, in a more limited way, every individual—is "chosen" or destined for some distinct purpose in advancing the designs of Providence.

The biblical proclamation of the Jews as the chosen people was made in the context of the pagan culture of that time. But even as early as the eighth century BCE, the prophet Amos proclaimed a more inclusive message:

> To Me, O Israelites, you are just like the Ethiopians—
> declares the LORD. True, I brought Israel up from the land
> of Egypt, but also the Philistines from Caphtor and the
> Arameans from Kir.
>
> *(Amos 9:7)*

The manner in which this chosenness is expressed in Jewish liturgy is instructive. Before the Torah is read in synagogue, the traditional blessing affirms chosenness in this way: "Blessed are You, Eternal One our God, Universal Creative Presence, Who has chosen us from among all Peoples and given us the Torah." In the Shabbat Kiddush, the blessing of the Sabbath wine, the chosen nature of the Jewish people is also expressed and defined: "… for You have chosen us, and sanctified us from among all Peoples, and have given us Your holy Sabbath with love and favor as our inheritance."

These traditional texts clearly affirm that Jews are chosen for the Jewish way. Many experience that way to be continually evolving, while others still look to the specifics in Torah for unchanging ritual and lifestyle requirements. No matter the degree of traditional adherence, Judaism is the way of Torah. It is for that way that Jews are chosen, and that is the path Jews choose.

SOCIAL REALITIES

However, there are some aspects of the Jewish experience that seem to create separation from others. Whether this separation expressly relates to exclusivity or not, it may give that impression to others.

Orthodox Jews, for example, usually cluster close to one another. Because they do not drive on the Sabbath, their participation in synagogue life requires that they live within walking distance of their house of worship. So Jewish neighborhoods are established—neighborhoods that usually reflect more of the Jewish culture than is visible elsewhere.

Ultra-Orthodox Jews tend to purposefully isolate themselves not only from the secular culture, but from non-Orthodox Jewish culture as well. They have strict limitations on what media are permitted, and even children's games need to have a Jewish focus. Exclusivity is a basic fact of life for these Jews, and they are happiest when not infringed upon by the surrounding culture. Even in Israel, where Judaism has greater visibility than in any other country on the planet, the ultra-Orthodox stand apart, and basically do not participate in activities outside their own relatively isolated communities.

Sometimes anti-Semitism makes the Jews an exclusive group. Although there are certainly Jews who flee from their identity in order to avoid such anti-Jewish sentiments, generally speaking, Jewish communities draw together more closely when attacked. Furthermore, anti-Jewish acts do not target observant Jews alone. In Hitler's attempted "Final Solution to the Jewish Problem," for instance, belief and observance had absolutely nothing to do with the definition of who was a Jew, and thus who was to be killed. Even when Jewish families had intermarried or converted to Christianity years earlier, if they had a certain percentage of Jewish blood, they were marked for extermination.

Perhaps the paranoia that surfaces in the Jewish community when Israel is publicly criticized can be understood in this historical context. The Jewish community is often unable to differentiate between criticism of Israel and criticism of Judaism and Jews. Part of what makes Jews exclusive as a community is the still-present awareness and fear of possible anti-Jewish sentiment and action.

THE TRIBAL NATURE OF JEWISH IDENTITY

The basically tribal nature of Jewish identity often appears as exclusivity. This identity is not predicated on the acceptance of a particular creed but rather on membership in what is essentially a family entity. In biblical times, religious identity flowed from the male head of a family. By the end of the biblical period, in the final centuries before the Common Era, Jewish identity became dependent on the identity of the mother. Only in Reform Judaism can a person claim Jewish identity through either a Jewish father or mother. Because Judaism represents a people, an ethnicity, as well as a religion, belief and observance alone are not sufficient criteria for Jewish identity.

Being a "member of the tribe" is a more substantial foundation of Jewish identity than any particular belief system or level of religious observance. It is fully possible to be an atheist and still be Jewish. One Jewish person can be observant of tradition and another can be totally unobservant, and both can be Jewish. Traditional Jews may not think much of their unobservant Jewish brothers or sisters, but there would be no question that they are both Jews.

Core Teachings and Healing

In Judaism, the core teaching of Oneness informs us that we are each a vehicle for a Universal Life Force that we can share to help and to heal.

We are all manifestations of One Life, each having the freedom to choose how we will embody that Life. We are free to support greater wholeness through loving and compassionate acts. And because we are free, we can also choose paths of greater pain, harming ourselves and others.

If there is One Life—a Oneness that manifests as everything that exists and infinitely more—then we might perceive ourselves as cells of a single Being. Each cell can work toward the health of that Being or not. In a human being, when a single cell, or a group of cells, begins to work against the health of the organism, we call that cancer. When individuals or a group perceive themselves and their needs to take priority over the needs of the entire community, they act as a cancer that begins to consume more than its share of the available resources. Although those individuals or that group might appear to grow stronger, it is at the cost of the greater organism. That kind of power begins, finally, to feed on itself.

When we are awake to our Oneness, ethical and compassionate actions come naturally. We recognize that caring for those in need is a way of more deeply caring for ourselves. We turn from a focus on self-gratification toward actions that support others as well as ourselves.

The Jewish prophets still convey this message across the span of centuries. The eighth-century BCE prophet Micah shared this recognition in words reflected by many other prophets and teachers in the evolution of Jewish tradition:

> It has already been told you, humankind, what is good, and what the Eternal asks of you: Only to do justly, to love kindness, and to walk with integrity with your God.
>
> *(Micah 6:8; author's translation)*

Each of us is challenged to attend more carefully to the core teachings of our faiths and to strive to go beyond recitation to demonstration. We are challenged to live from our core teachings so that others will know our teachings through our acts. This is the possibility and this is the promise toward which we travel together.

Exclusivity in Christianity
Personal Reflections

My conditioning concerning exclusivity and triumphalism as a Christian in America has two sources: the teachings of the Christian church and the cultural sensibility that America is the new Promised Land. It is hard to know where to draw the line between the idea that Christianity is the only way to healing and the idea that the United States as a Christian nation deserves to triumph over the rest of the world. Certainly our nationalism has contributed to Christianity's exclusive claims.

When those first Europeans came to North America, there was a real sense of making another crossing into a Promised Land. The Atlantic became the new Jordan and the wilderness of this continent seemed to have been promised by God. This contributed to the persecution and slaughter of native peoples already here, and it eventually turned into the concept of Manifest Destiny, the idea that our Christianity, along with our American citizenship, made us deserving of triumph—an idea that could not be further from the Gospel of Jesus. Still it was that sort of cultural sensibility—the idea that Christianity is the only way to salvation and that other people, having chosen other paths, were deserving of their fate—that shaped my Christian thinking.

When I was about six years old, I was sitting in a pew at church with friends on a Sunday morning. My mother was singing in the choir, and my father was helping to serve communion. When the older man who passed out the tray of neatly cut-up pieces of bread reached my seat, I instinctively put out my hand to take a piece. The man, a retired Baptist minister, reached over and slapped my hand. I don't remember exactly what he said, but the meaning was clear. At that moment, I was to be excluded from the elements of the sacrament of communion.

I don't remember ever having a conversation about this with my parents before this incident because, if I had, I might have known better than to reach for the bread. In fairness to the elderly gentleman who slapped my hand, he was simply abiding by the principle that communion should be available only to those who had passed through the ritual and process of confirmation. Confirmation represented a cognitive awareness of the meaning of being a Christian and was made available in a special class to youth between the ages of twelve and sixteen. The word *confirmation* is a reference to the confirmation of the vows taken on one's behalf in the sacrament of baptism. One must be baptized to be a Christian, and, in my tradition, a person is baptized as an infant and then given a more intellectual access to Jesus and his ministry in adolescence.

What upset and embarrassed me was the harshness and the absolute inflexibility of the moment. I received a clear message that you could be a Christian only by adhering to a strict set of passages and beliefs. And that adherence made us *different* from other people. And, perhaps more to the point, it made us different in a country where the triumph of American nationalism in the United States was, at times, almost indistinguishable from Protestant Christianity. My manifest destiny was to be a successful Christian in a successful Protestant Christian nation. The familiar hymn that begins, "Onward Christian soldiers, marching as to war" is a testament to the cultural sensibility I am describing. The natural triumph of Christianity was to be supported by an authorization to, in a militant way, force the belief in Christian triumph onto others. Their refusal would result in an unhappy fate. Even as a small child, I can remember feeling that there was something deeply wrong with that attitude.

Scriptural and Institutional Support for Exclusivity

There are many verses in the Christian Scriptures supporting the notion that Christianity is the only way to salvation and healing. The most influential of these verses is found in the Gospel of John, where Jesus speaks to his disciples before his arrest, during the Passover meal now known as the Last Supper:

> Thomas said to him, "Lord we do not know where you are going. How can we know the way?" Jesus said to him, "I am the way, the truth and the life. No one comes to the Father except by me. If you know me, you will know my Father also. From now on, you do know him and have seen him."
>
> *(John 14:5–7)*

I believe that those verses have provided most of the energy and ambition for those wishing to proclaim that Christianity is the only way to salvation.

But other verses underscore those sentiments. For example, in the book of Acts, which recounts the experience of the early church, Peter and John are arrested by religious authorities in Jerusalem for preaching about the resurrection of the dead. Peter then cites Jesus as the authority for their preaching:

> This Jesus is the stone that was rejected by you, the builders; it has become the cornerstone. There is salvation in no one else, for there is no other name under heaven given among mortals by which we must be saved.
>
> *(Acts 4:11–12)*

In the letter to the church at Ephesus, written by Paul (or by one of Paul's followers), we find this familiar verse: "One Lord, one faith, one baptism, one God and Father of all, who is above all and through all and in all" (Ephesians 4:5). The letter attempts to convey a vision of what the church should be about.

In the Gospel of Luke, we find: "Whoever listens to you, listens to me, and whoever rejects you rejects me, and whoever rejects me rejects the one who sent me" (10:16).

In the Gospel of John, we read: "Those who believe in him are not condemned; but those who do not believe are condemned already, because they have not believed in the name of the only Son of God" (3:18).

These verses represent a sensibility spread throughout the Christian Scriptures that gained traction as the Gospels were being written down in Greek between 70 and 100 CE.

Practices of the church that reflect the sensibility expressed in the verses above are many and horrible. Individual churches, and indeed individual persons, committed acts against Jews (and later against Muslims), acts that were wrongly justified by the idea of the triumph of Christianity on the world stage. These practices became known collectively as anti-Semitism, the repudiation of Judaism and the persecution of Jews simply because they were Jewish. The justification for this was based on the texts noted above, as well as the need to be correct. But supersessionism, the conviction that Christianity takes the place of Judaism, became a standard part of Christian thought and practice and led to profound hatred and violence. Later, anti-Semitism rooted in supersessionism turned into the repudiation of anyone who was not Christian and then anyone who wasn't a "true" Christian. We have a romantic sense that there was a unified Christianity right from the beginning. But today scholars suggest that there were numerous versions of Christianity, many versions of who Jesus was and what he taught, many versions of liturgy for Christian worship, and many versions of songs and hymns that were sung during worship. Around 180 CE a book titled *Adversus Haereses* (Against Heresies) appeared, written by Irenaeus, bishop of Lugdunum in Gaul of the Roman Empire (today Lyons in France). His aim was to find a way to determine the path of "true" Christianity, specifically as a defense against Gnosticism. Some would say that Christian orthodoxy began with this attempt.

The consequence of Irenaeus's inquiry was a drastic reinforcement of the idea that Christianity was the only path to salvation and that Christian orthodoxy was the only true Christian path to salvation. Ultimately, this became known as *"extra ecclesiam nulla salu*—outside the church there is no salvation." Of course, *ecclesiam* refers to not just any church, but the one *true* church. The irony is that the prefix *ek* in *ecclesiam* refers to a "gathering in." So the Latin means literally "outside the realm where nothing is outside." In fact, as Wallace Alston points out in his book *The Church,* in the broadest sense the word *church* points to all of humanity and that the establishment of the church is, de facto, a second creation.[1] But because of its exclusivist sensibility, the institution of the church has interpreted this to mean that all people should be Christians. The force of this conviction has colored much of Christian history with suffering.

The inclusivity that Jesus taught in his first sermon at Nazareth (Luke 4:16–30), suggesting that Jews are not the only people chosen by and loved by God, is in radical contrast to the later exclusive actions of the Christian church over its entire history.

The first historical example of large-scale Christian exclusivity is the gradual expulsion of Jews from Europe between 1100 and 1650. In 1290, Edward I of England issued an Edict of Expulsion, forcing the small Jewish population in England to leave. As they left, the king appropriated their wealth.

Later came the expulsion of Jews and Muslims from Spain in 1492 by Ferdinand and Isabella (the more important reason to remember 1492), which resulted in the Spanish Inquisition, or the Tribunal of the Holy Office of the Inquisition. The Inquisition was actually instituted in 1478 as a way of monitoring the sincerity of Jews and Muslims who had converted to Christianity. It was not until 1492 that Jews and Muslims were ordered to convert or leave Spain. The pain caused by this action can hardly be understood by Christians today. But it is important to remember that the impetus and justification for the Inquisition was that deep sense that Christianity was the only way to salvation. That conviction was used to justify suffering on a magnitude that simply cannot be calculated.

In addition to the expulsion of Jews from Europe during the Middle Ages and the Inquisition in Spain, the Crusades represent another horrific use of Christianity to justify violence, torture, and the acquisition of wealth at the expense of non-Christians. In his book *The Crusades through Arab Eyes*, Amin Maalouf uses texts from that time to show that the European Christians coming to regain "control" of the "Holy Land" (a term designated by Christians for Christians and excluding Jews and Muslims) not only used violence against Jews along the way, against Muslims living in Turkey, Palestine, and Egypt, but even against Christians who were living in the Middle East.[2] They were after power and money and used the triumphal teachings of the Christian church to support their cause. The ambitions behind the Crusades were adventure and the recovery of control over the trade routes that intersected in the Holy Land. But this tragic use of Christianity as a justification for or an authority to commit crimes against non-Christians was only gaining momentum in the Middle and late Middle Ages.

In the aftermath of World War I, when Germany was totally humiliated by the Treaty of Versailles, it is not difficult to see how a charismatic figure like Adolf Hitler could stir national consciousness and start to rebuild German self-esteem by declaring Germany an "Aryan" nation, a nation in which Christianity would be the only acceptable religion. Hitler himself believed that he was acting in accord with God's purposes: "Therefore, I believe today that I am acting in the sense of the Almighty Creator: By warding off the Jews I am fighting for the Lord's work."[3] He was using the history of the repudiation of Judaism to support his vision of Germany as a nation of superpeople.

Beginning with the legalization of Christianity by Constantine, Christianity historically merged with governments of power and domination systems to become the authority by which violence, hatred, exclusion, and racism could be perpetrated, justified, and supported. If Christianity were truly understood to be the only way, other ways of living had to be wrong. Again, what could be further from the substance of Jesus's teachings?

This shift from a communal understanding of the teachings of Jesus as a way, to a merging with political domination to become an authoritative method to coerce and, yes, even enslave, is not unique in religious history. In fact, the traditions of Abraham have seen spiritual awareness slip into an ego-centered numbness over and over again. But for Christianity, the experience of slipping into numbness has resulted in untold suffering and violence.

Commentary on Exclusivity

Scripture does not give us a complete or accurate picture of what happened immediately after the death of Jesus. If we read it literally, it seems that there was always an antagonistic relationship between Christians and "the Jews" (a recurring phrase in each of the four Gospels). However, not only were Jesus and his disciples Jews, Jesus himself was a Jewish teacher, a rabbi. While a handful of wealthy Jews associated with the administration of the Temple in Jerusalem felt their positions threatened by the teachings of Jesus, the real threat presented by Jesus was to the imperial aspirations of Rome. Jesus preached about a kingdom—a word that pointed to current reality as well as to the future. At its heart, the word *Kingdom* suggests a state of being that provides no space for any empire. The kingdom of Jesus's teaching actually contained no earthly king. It was communal, cooperative, and collaborative.

So, by the time the scriptures were being written down (ca. 70 CE for Mark and up to 100 CE for John), the argument about whether or not Jesus was the Messiah was in full force. There were Jewish Christians, Gentile Christians, and Jews—Jews who did not accept Jesus as the One they were hoping for. (In Hebrew the word *mashiach,* or Messiah, means "one anointed or chosen by God for the purpose of helping to bring healing to the world." In Greek it is *Christos,* from which we get the word *Christ*.) Over time, Jews became the theological enemy of Christians, a polarity that eventually morphed into the violent repudiation and subjugation of Jews by Christians. So it is easy to see how a verse such as "I am the way, the truth, and the life. No one comes to God except by me" (John 14:6b) got into John's Gospel.

It is my sense that Jesus was a spiritual teacher, one who would never have taught from that narrow place of a personal *I.* His teachings had a cosmic, spiritual, and inclusive sensibility. I believe that when he is depicted as speaking about himself, in an ego-based manner, that depiction is the result of the early church misunderstanding his words and their context. The broader and more universal teachings of Jesus were rooted in the oneness of Judaism and in the notion of unconditional love, as in the verse from Matthew, "Love your enemies and pray for those who persecute you …" (5:44). The goal of Jesus's teachings was to make oneness real and to illuminate compassion as the act by which it comes to life (as in the story of the Good Samaritan in Luke 10:25–37).

Rabbi Ted has pointed out that in Hebrew the verb *to be* is often understood but not written or spoken. I like to think that the origin of "I am the way, the truth, and the life" came from a saying in Hebrew that might have been "I AM *is* the way, the truth and the life." The name of God revealed to Moses in the famous burning bush episode is *I AM*. God is Being. The verse might originally have been about God and not about Jesus. Jesus often spoke of God. "No one comes to God except by me" seems to be raw testimony to that desperate urge to claim exclusive religious and spiritual authority. All the other verses from scripture that support an exclusivist sensibility about Christianity are there, I am convinced, simply to provide a platform for that conviction.

Core Teachings and Healing

The teachings of Jesus that emphasize unconditional love point to a Oneness that is the antithesis of exclusivity. As a rabbi, Jesus's sense of Oneness was central to his teachings. Without conditions, love has no boundaries, no reason to fence itself off, no need to feel different or superior, and no sensibility of separateness. That historic tribal sense that "we" are here and "they" are there, a sense that still contributes to the polarized cultures in today's world, can be overcome by an understanding and incorporation of unconditional love.

The false sense of superiority that both individuals and institutions harbor is created by the conditions of love. When we say, "We are better than they are," we are saying that we love ourselves more than we love others, because we believe we are more worthy of love than the Other. But from a spiritual point of view, we are all the same. We share an equal sense of worth, a worth with enormous positive value. Unconditional love erases those boundaries by affirming that there is no need to define our values as superior to others.

The difficulty that remains is that we have no real or shared sense of the meaning of unconditional love. The word *love* has so many meanings in our world, but among all the meanings, we rarely find that sense of the unconditional.

Interfaith dialogue has helped us to see that while unconditional love undergirds Christianity, it suffuses all spiritual traditions and can serve as a basis for healing in our world. Such dialogue can lead to a deeper understanding of unconditional love as well as the recognition of how its meaning and blessings can help heal our troubled world.

Exclusivity in Islam

Personal Reflections

One of the things I most treasured about Islam when I was growing up was the openhearted way with which it was practiced in my family. The Qur'an spoke so sweetly of "spacious paths" (e.g., 71:18–19), and my parents and grandparents walked those paths with such love that I, too, embraced my ancestral religion with all my heart. Eagerly I devoured the words of the Qur'an, which my deeply spiritual grandfather said were the very words of God, and with joy I absorbed their meaning as taught by my beloved parents. Our focus in those days was the message of divine spaciousness and inclusivity in the Holy Book. The loving heart of God embraces all humankind, I was told, and from an early age I was privileged to see just how diverse humanity is because my father was a professional diplomat, and we were posted to countries all over the world during my childhood. Wherever we lived—Pakistan, India, Burma, Iran, Turkey, Egypt, Saudi Arabia, Sudan, Germany, Italy, and Canada—my parents encouraged me and my siblings to get to know the local children and celebrate their sacred festivals whether in mosque, church, synagogue, or temple.

There was never any question about the core religion I would follow, but it gave me great pleasure to know that, as a Muslim, I shared a deep reverence for the prophet Abraham with my Jewish friends and for Jesus with my Christian friends. What joy it gave me to gaze upon the Kaaba on those starry nights in Mecca! That cubic stone structure is the symbolic House of God—the same God worshipped by my friends in all three Abrahamic faiths! We had our own tradition about the Kaaba—that it was was built by Adam, founder of the human race, and then rebuilt by the prophet Ibrahim (Abraham) and his first son, Ismail (Ishmael), progenitor of Islam—but as the House of God it belonged to everyone. My heart, like the heart of Allah, expanded to include all my Abrahamic sisters and brothers all over the world.

And then one day my idealistic vision was shattered. It happened when I learned that people were being stopped at checkpoints on the way to Mecca and Medina. The ostensible reason was to preserve the purity and sanctity of these two sacred cities by banning the curious non-Muslim. A high-ranking Saudi imam said the prohibition was rooted in a Qur'anic verse: "O you who believe! Truly the pagans are unclean; so let them not, after this year of theirs, approach the Sacred Mosque" (9:28). But this verse, as I now know, refers specifically and only to some members of the seventh-century Quraysh tribe and their allies, who were opposed to the then-new religion of Islam. Disregarding that fact, the Wahabi clergy of Saudi Arabia took a literalist view and extended the word *idolaters* to encompass all non-Muslims. Not for them the spacious, inclusive policies of the Prophet Muhammad! In his time, the Prophet received many delegations of Jews and Christians for conversations and negotiations that sometimes were lengthy and extended into their service times. At those times, the Prophet invited his guests to perform the Shabbat and Sunday services in the mosque, which was considered "simply a place consecrated to God."

This was my first inkling that not all was sweetness and light in the Holy Qur'an, but it was not my last. Over the next few years I learned that some verses were "difficult" and "awkward" and lent themselves to a variety of interpretations, not all of them gracious.

Of course, I felt cheated and disillusioned, but at the same time I was intrigued by this new concept called "interpretation." From my mother I learned to ask not what the Qur'an has to say, but who is interpreting what the Qur'an has to say.

I had more reason to question interpretations of the Qur'an when, as a teenager, I became aware of the pain that religious exclusion can inflict on minorities inside the fold of Islam. In Pakistan I had some friends who were Ahmadis, members of a Muslim sect founded in the nineteenth century by Mirza Ghulam Ahmad to revive and rejuvenate Islam. To Muslim conservatives, the Ahmadi belief in any kind of prophetic role for their founder is sacrilegious because in the Qur'an, the Prophet Muhammad is the "seal" of the prophets. Thus, even though those in the Ahmadiyya community follow the precepts of mainstream Islam and believe in Muhammad as the final law-bearing Prophet of humanity (a distinction is made between a prophet and a law-bearing Prophet, such as Moses, Jesus, and Muhammad, who are also Messengers), in Pakistan they have been excommunicated and persecuted as heretics, a cause of great sorrow and fear to my Ahmadi friends. A Sufi teacher once remarked to me that if the Ahmadis are mistaken in their belief, this "sin" is placed in their ledger, not ours. Why do we get so agitated about this?

These same Pakistani clerics would gladly have excommunicated the 15 percent of Muslims called Shia, whom they also accuse of blasphemy and sacrilege. That story goes back to the seventh century, when the young Islamic community was sundered by a dispute about choosing a leader after the Prophet died. One group, calling themselves adherents of the Prophet's *Sunnah*, or "tradition," said the leader should be chosen by consensus. The others wanted to choose a blood relative of the Prophet and threw their support behind Hazrat Ali, Muhammad's cousin and son-in-law. The "Sunnah" group (called Sunnis) won the power, but not without vicious battles and intrigues against the Shia (Party) of Ali, culminating in the massacre of the Prophet's family. To this day, the rift between Sunni and Shia Muslims causes suffering and lamentation wherever the two denominations fight each other over limited political and economic resources.

Although Sunni myself, I remember being quite shocked one day when my Qur'an teacher in Pakistan launched into a tirade against the Shias. Standing there in the turban and sash of a religious leader, he condemned the Shias as heretics and declared their prayers null and void. How, I thought, can a man of God and a representative of the Qur'an be so narrow-minded and uncharitable to his fellow Muslims? When I think of him now, a verse from the Sufi mystic Kabir comes to mind: "The Yogi comes along in his famous orange. But if inside he is colorless, then what?"[4]

In my life story, I have to acknowledge my conditioning: a fascination with the universal themes in the Qur'an and the life of Muhammad; a starry-eyed love of Islamic mystics, especially the thirteenth-century sage Rumi; deep-seated suspicions of ahadith (plural of *hadith*, which means "a saying of the Prophet Muhammad") that are not consistent with the spirit of the Qur'an; and a special distaste for narrow-minded clerics. On this last point I want to say that I have been privileged to know several Muslim clerics of dazzling devotion and heart-melting compassion. I am only sad that their inner light seems unable to outshine the shadows cast by sectarian and misogynistic clerics, who pretend to speak for the faith I hold so dear.

Scriptural and Institutional Support for Exclusivity

There are a number of Qur'anic verses that support the exclusivist tendencies of literalists. To start with, the Qur'an does acknowledge that there is nothing new in the revelations given to the Prophet Muhammad; similar spiritual light and guidance appear in the Hebrew and Christian Scriptures (e.g., 5:44; 6:92). But then it goes on to say that some Jews and Christians have tampered with their divine texts (e.g., 5:13–14), whereas the verses of the Qur'an are authentic and uncorrupted (e.g., 32:2; 39:23). Such statements are an open invitation to the untamed ego to say, "My religion and my scriptures are better than yours." Such claims only serve to inflate the ego and create what Sufi teachers call "religious vertigo."

The Qur'an is particularly insulting to those Jews who transgress against divine law. God transformed them into apes and swine, it says (5:60), and commanded them to be "despised and rejected" (2:65; 7:166). Summarizing the faithlessness of the Jewish transgressors, the Qur'an declares that they deserve whatever punishment God metes out: "They drew on themselves the wrath of God. This because they went on rejecting the Signs of God and slaying His Messengers without just cause. This because they rebelled and went on transgressing" (2:61).

Christians seem to fare better in the Qur'an, at least in terms of personal morality, but it claims that to believe that Jesus is the incarnate Son of God is blasphemy. Jesus is deeply revered as a prophet and is called the "Spirit of God" in the Qur'an, but he is called a mere mortal, "no more than an Apostle" (5:75) born of human flesh. A central tenet of Islam is that God "neither begets nor is begotten" (112:3). Thus Christians who claim that Jesus is divine are "deluded away from the truth" (5:75); it is a blasphemy, a thing "most monstrous ... that they should invoke a son for God Most Gracious" (19:89–91).

One verse often quoted at me in interfaith gatherings is the command, "Take not the Jews and Christians for your friends and protectors for they are but friends and protectors to one another" (5:51). Another, cited as proof that Muslims believe their faith is superior to all others, is this: "So whoever seeks religion other than Islam, it will not be accepted from him, and he will be one of the losers in the Hereafter" (3:85). Here I can only reassert that the operative principle in these discussions is not what the Qur'an says but who is interpreting the words and with what agenda.

Some interpretations of the Qur'an reflect institutional bias, but the historical results of this biased thinking are mixed. Relations between Muslims and Jews were not entirely comfortable in the early years, but during the Golden Age (the ninth to the twelfth centuries) and the Ottoman Empire (the fourteenth to the early twentieth centuries), things were relatively peaceful. Relations between Muslims and Christians were initially peaceful, but later became fraught with struggles for political power, and the Crusades resulted in senseless killing on both sides of the battlefield. Theologically, however, all three faiths shared a commitment to monotheism and, during the Ottoman Empire, relative peace reigned among them.

All this changed in the twentieth century after the fall of the Ottoman Empire, the fight against colonialism, and, especially, after the creation of the State of Israel. Enraged by what they saw as a land grab, the Arab nations swore enmity to "the Zionist Jews" and their supporters in the "colonial West" who created this political disaster. Doing what humans seem to do quite naturally, they combed their sacred scriptures for proof of their own moral superiority, and there it was. Miraculously, fabricated anti-Jewish ahadith also began to appear. One particular hadith says, "The Day of Judgment will not come about until Muslims fight the Jews [killing the Jews] when the Jew will hide behind stone and trees. The stone and trees will say, 'O Muslims, O Abdullah, there is a Jew behind me, come and kill him.'"[5]

Sometimes governments and religious institutions dovetail their efforts to preserve exclusivity. In Saudi Arabia, for example, monarchy and clerics have tampered with the Sura Fateha, the opening chapter of the Qur'an. In this universal prayer for guidance on the straight path to God, humanity pleads not to be counted "of those who have earned your wrath, nor of those who go astray." But the Saudi establishment has sullied the purity of this beautiful prayer by inserting the word *Jews* in the phrase "those who have earned your wrath" and *Christians* in the phrase "those who go astray." These insertions are utterly contrary to the belief that the Qur'an is the uncorrupted word of God.

The institution of Islam also protects its dominance by enforcing strict penalties for the crime of blasphemy against the Muslim faith or the Prophet Muhammad. In Pakistan, a Christian woman has been condemned to death for such a crime. The governor of Punjab, Salman Taseer, advocated the repeal of blasphemy laws because they are misused to oppress minorities and was rewarded by death at the hands of his own guard, who calls himself "a slave of the Prophet." More than five hundred Pakistani clerics and jurists have praised the murderer as a hero, and his act as a sacred deed.

Internecine exclusivity is also a problem in Islam. Sunnis and Shias all read the same Holy Book and follow the same precepts, but they almost always pray in separate mosques. In extreme cases, they also bomb each other's mosques. Even in death they may refuse to associate with each other: Shias and Sunnis are sometimes buried in separate cemeteries.

Does God have any bylaws about who can enter heaven? Do you have to be a Muslim? The Qur'an insists that neither gender nor religion determines your placement in heaven. Essentially, the password is *righteous deeds*. Nevertheless, many Islamic institutions cite a hadith about two frightful angels, named Munkar and Nakir, who visit the gravesite of a person freshly laid to rest and ask three questions: "Who is your Lord? Who is your Prophet? What is your religion?" Should your answer be wrong, you will be tormented in your grave and in the fires of hell.

Commentary on Exclusivity

In a sweet example of poetic justice, the same Holy Book that is abused by Islamic chauvinism also provides the remedy for this spiritual disease. The second-most-used word in the Qur'an, after Allah, is *ilm*, the Arabic word for "knowledge." The Qur'an advises us to pray, "O God, advance me in knowledge," and the Prophet daily prayed, "O God, may I see things as they really are." In that spirit, let us reexamine some of the troublesome verses cited earlier to see if we can heal the wounds caused by ego-driven misinterpretation.

"So whoever seeks religion other than Islam it will not be accepted from him and he will be one of the losers in the Hereafter" (3:85). Historically speaking, Muhammad received this revelation when Islam was not yet formalized as a religion. The word *islam*, from the Arabic root meaning "surrender," "peace," and "wholeness" (akin to the meanings of the Hebrew word *shalom*), refers to the path of becoming whole by surrendering one's ego to God in peace. It has nothing to do with the specific religion of Muslims. In that sense, the Qur'an calls Abraham the "first Muslim" and considers all the biblical prophets to be Muslims because they brought a heart "turned in devotion to God" (50:33). Even more crucial than the historical context of this revelation is its textual context. Those who harp on this verse tend to ignore the verse just before it, which happens to be one of the most inclusive verses in the Qur'an. It affirms belief in the revelations sent "to Abraham and Ishmael and Isaac and Jacob and their descendants and that which has been vouchsafed to Moses and Jesus," and further adds, "We make no distinction between any of them. And unto Him do we surrender ourselves" (3:84). Thus by reading the verse in context, we can discern its true meaning. Far from preaching exclusivity, it exhorts all humanity to bring God into the center of our lives.

"Take not the Jews and Christians as your friends and protectors for they are but friends and protectors to one another" (5:51) is a good example of the need to make a distinction between particular and universal verses. This verse was revealed at a particular point in history when some Jewish and Christian tribes had treaties of alliance with Muslims, and this included military support against attack from the Meccan Quraysh tribe, but according to Muslims, they wavered on their commitments. Thus it should not be read as a categorical condemnation of all Jews and Christians. Just a few lines later is a verse affirming the goodness of other believers: "Those who believe [in the Qur'an], those who follow the Jewish [Scriptures], and the Sabians, and the Christians—any who believe in Allah and the Last Day, and work righteousness—on them shall be no fear, nor shall they grieve" (5:69).

Now, what about those *apes and swine* verses? Again, progressive Islamic theologians say this is an example of particular versus universal verses. *Apes and swine* refer to the corruption of some Jews at a certain point in history, and the Qur'an clearly says "Not all of them are alike ... of the People of the Book are a portion that stand for the right ... they are in the ranks of the righteous" (3:113–114). Furthermore, the epithet was hurled not only at Jews but also at Muslims. A hadith says the Prophet used these words to warn his own people that if they transgress exceedingly, Allah will let the mountain fall on them, and "He will transform the rest of them into monkeys and pigs ... till the day of Resurrection."[6] Even so, we have to acknowledge that the insults are hurtful and that the verses are easily misused. It ill befits any of us to use derogatory language about our fellow human beings.

How do we bring a higher understanding to shine on these verses? If we allow ourselves to move beyond our biases, we might see these verses as a warning that anyone who habitually transgresses the bounds of what is right is less than human in the eyes of God. When we manipulate divine laws or put words in the mouth of our Prophet by fabricating ahadith to support our own self-interest, are we not acting like clever monkeys?

"For behold, thy Sustainer knows best as to who strays from His path, and best knows He as to who are the right guided," says the Qur'an (16:125), and it repeatedly adjures Muslims to be gracious in word and deed with all People of the Book. "Dispute ye not with the People of the Book ... but say 'We believe in the Revelation which has come down to us and in that which came down to you: our God and your God is One; and it is to Him we bow'" (29:46). Thus when we criticize the beliefs or practices of other religious communities, we are setting ourselves above the God who made us all. It is human folly to claim that our religion is the only way to reach God and our scripture is the only authentic word of God. Though the Qur'an suggests that some Christians and Jews have corrupted divine revelations, have we Muslims not done the same by interpreting Qur'anic verses to suit our own convenience? The Qur'an calls all of us—Jews, Christians, and Muslims—"People of the Book." The operative phrase here is *the Book*: one book, of which the Qur'an is a one-third installment.

Core Teachings and Healing

For the Muslim community, there is the difficult but necessary work of closing the gap between the Qur'anic ideal and the political reality on the ground, which is often diametrically opposed to the spirit and teachings of the Qur'an and the Prophet. It behooves us all to reflect on a historic document called "The Constitution of Medina." Created by the Prophet in 622 CE, this momentous document declares, "the Jews shall practice their religion as freely as the Muslims ... shall be protected from all insults and vexations ... [and] they shall have an equal right with our own people." In a separate pact with Christians, Muhammad promised that he would safeguard "their lives, their religion, and their property" and that there would be "no interference with the practice of their faith or their observances; nor any change in their rights or privileges." By honoring our Prophet's pledge and walking the spacious paths of the Qur'an, each of us can do our part to heal the wounds of exclusivity so that together we shall have our reward with the one God who sustains and cherishes us all.

KNOW THYSELF

Religious defensiveness and exclusivity are altogether human manifestations of the need to build ourselves up by tearing someone else down. It is not God or our religion that is bruised when someone criticizes our faith; it is our own insecure ego. Our need to own the best religion reflects the desire to be mama's dearest child, teacher's favorite student, and God's most special friend. And it is heartbreaking, because it betrays our ignorance of just how special we already are in the eyes of God.

The Qur'an teaches that we humans are fashioned "in the best of molds" (95:4) and God "breathed into him something of His Spirit" (32:9). So why can we not see ourselves and each other through kinder, gentler eyes? Perhaps it's because, out of a divine design, we also have what the Qur'an calls a "slinking whisperer" (114:4), which skews our vision and tempts us to act in ways that feed our egos to the detriment of our higher selves. The "slinking whisperer" is the devil's advocate, the voice that tests us and, in turn, helps us develop our own divine qualities of compassion, awareness, humility, patience, sincerity, and truth. We learn through opposites. Our work in both our personal and sectarian lives is to cultivate self-awareness and compassion so that we can evolve into the fullness of our being.

It is the role of religion to offer insights and prescriptions for this inner work, and Islam is no exception. The Qur'an specifies three stages of the ego that we are asked to transform (12:53, 75:2, 89:27). In the first stage, we learn to transform the ego from a "commanding master" to an "assistant"; in the second stage the ego learns about the power and beauty of making good choices; and in the third stage, the ego is at peace because it is aligned with the soul. From a compassionate, wise, and spacious being will flow compassionate, wise, and spacious actions. The untamed ego prefers to debate about religion, fight over it, and even kill for it. This untamed part of us will do everything but live the faith. The ego that works to transform itself according to the Qur'anic ideals of compassion, love, and authenticity has no need to see itself as separate from or superior to any other of God's precious human beings.

In an exquisite moment of epiphany, the Prophet declared, "I am He and He is I—except that I am I and He is He!" That is true of every human being. Within each of us is the spark of divinity, the breath of God. Our essential nature is boundlessly spacious, gracious, generous, and inclusive. Once we connect to our essential nature, we shall usher in the freedom of our true Self. But to get there we need to let go of our individual narratives and conditionings, which make us judgmental, biased, and exclusive. How do we do this? In all traditions, a primary step is the same: Get to know yourself. The Buddha said, "Know others and you become wise; know yourself and you become enlightened." And the Prophet Muhammad said, "Know thyself and you shall know thy Sustainer." By continuously shining the light of compassionate awareness on our intentions and behaviors, we reduce the shadows of our conditionings and move into the light of our higher selves.

Concluding Comments

It is crucial to recognize the tendencies toward exclusivity in our personal lives as well as in our traditions. The more aware we are of the source of that exclusivity, the better able we will be to avoid the pitfalls of such beliefs.

Unless we transcend our personal and institutional exclusivities, a peaceful pluralistic society is simply not possible. We can be deeply committed to our faith without demanding that it's the only way.

Sharing Our Stories

When Ted invited Jamal to share the Shabbat service at his synagogue three days after 9/11, one of the unforeseen consequences for Ted was his decision to wear a *kippah*, the Jewish skullcap (better known as a *yarmulke*), all the time. He had worn it during prayer and teaching for many years, but now he wanted to be as public with his identity as Jamal was with his. In those early tense days for American Muslims, he knew it was important for people to see a Jew and a Muslim walking peacefully together.

Being a "public Jew" brought Ted some new kinds of attention and gave him an opportunity to deliberately step into his fears of being targeted as a Jew. Few Jews in the area of Seattle in which he lives walk around with little hats on their heads, and he found that people in the stores and restaurants he frequented got to know who he was very quickly. More than one homeless person asking for money on the street made a point of coming over and greeting him with a hearty "Shalom!"

One of the stores that Ted patronized regularly was never open on Sundays because it was owned by a deeply committed evangelical Christian. Sometimes Ted was aware of a little tension in the air between them but, for a long time, neither of them said anything to the other about their differences. Occasionally, Ted would hear the storeowner talking to another customer about his church activities but, while he wondered if the owner had any feelings about having a Jew as a regular customer, the man maintained a polite distance between them.

Then, one afternoon the owner stepped through the wall of silence.

"You know," he said, putting a friendly hand on Ted's shoulder, "your God and my God are the same God." Ted smiled and nodded. How wonderful that the regular presence of a practicing Jew in his store had caused this devout evangelical to think about things and arrive at this conclusion. But before Ted could say anything in response, the storeowner suddenly continued, "But that Allah guy is somebody else!"

Ted was startled and saddened by this remark. And he knew that to try to talk the man out of what was clearly a deeply held belief was not something that could happen in passing in a crowded store. At that moment, the only thing that he could say was, "There is only one God, and this is something that needs a longer conversation."

But that longer conversation has not yet happened. The two men are not friends. The owner had not asked for Ted's opinion, and he rapidly turned away to another customer after Ted's response. On Ted's next visit to the store, the slight chill in the air had turned to frost, and he knew that there was no opening for that longer conversation. He still goes to the store occasionally but visits it less and less often.

When Ted told Don and Jamal about this experience, Don was reminded of the time he had been writing in a coffee shop one afternoon, with a copy of our first book, *Getting to the Heart of Interfaith*, lying on the table beside his computer. A middle-aged woman approached him. She pointed to the book and shook her head.

"Islam," she announced in a loud voice, "is a bad religion. Muslims are evil and violent people, and that's what their religion teaches them to be!"

Heads turned, and Don attempted to engage her in conversation.

"I've been studying Islam," he said, "and working closely with a Muslim for several years. I have learned something very different."

"You're wrong!" she shouted. "It's an evil and violent religion! If you think anything else, then you are a fool!" And, with that, she turned and practically ran out of the coffee shop, as if merely being around someone who felt differently about Muslims was too upsetting to tolerate.

Don looked around and met the eyes of many of those who had witnessed the encounter. And in that moment, he knew that there was an understanding shared without words, a recognition that anger made communication impossible, that deeply held prejudices are not always amenable to conversation, that the force of certainty can inhibit dialogue.

In our work together, we recognize that we will not always be able to forge meaningful dialogue with those who oppose what we are doing. When Ted was in seminary, there was a Jesuit there studying the Hebrew Bible. He shared a religious distinction that Ted has never forgotten. "There's a difference between lobster theology and backbone theology," the young priest told him. "Lobster theology is tough on the outside but mushy on the inside, so it has to fight off any conflicting viewpoints. There is no chance for meaningful dialogue. Backbone theology is more yielding, it can bend and still retain its integrity. Disagreement and opposing viewpoints are possible. Real dialogue can occur."

Perhaps it's best summed up in a teaching Imam Jamal got from his parents: "Blessed are the flexible, for they will never be bent out of shape."

Questions for Discussion

- If you were asked to choose a religion besides your own, which tradition would you choose? Why would you make that choice?

- Is there a religious tradition that you feel uneasy about? What makes you uneasy? What are your sources for information about that religion? Are those sources reliable? How would you go about acquiring an appreciative understanding of that faith? How would you go about connecting with a member of that tradition?

- Sometimes people of different faiths can work together on social justice or earth-care projects. If you were working with someone who believed her religion held the only truth, would that bother you? Would that stand in the way of your collaboration with her? Would you raise the issue? What outcome would you desire?

Spiritual Practices

From Jewish Tradition

Meditate on the Hebrew, "*Adonai Hu ha-Elohim*" (1 Kings 18:39) or an English equivalent, "The One indwells in all." Originally spoken by the children of Israel when the prophet Elijah demonstrated the power of their God, this verse is traditionally recited as a meditation and spoken at the moment of death. We are called to remember that everyone and everything that exists is an expression of the One Life we share.

From Christian Tradition

Meditate on the verse, "I AM is the way, the truth, and the life" (John 14:6). Remember that the name of God revealed to Moses is I AM, and that the present tense of the verb *to be* is understood but not written in biblical Hebrew, so I believe this verse means "I AM *is* the way," rather than simply "I am the way." Jesus was a profound spiritual teacher, so it is most likely that he was speaking of this shared I AM, rather than speaking from his separate self.

From Islamic Tradition

Meditate on the verse, "Everywhere you turn is the face of Allah" (2:115). Close your eyes, focus on your nostrils, and be mindful of your in-breath and your out-breath. Make a prayerful intention that your inhalation and exhalation are joyously connecting you to Divinity inside and outside of you.

Chapter Two

Violence

Justifying Brutality in the Name of Faith

Violence is one of the most dramatic and tragic consequences of exclusivity. When we feel ours is the only way, it is easy to dehumanize the other, leading to brutality from the darkest places of our being.

The issue becomes more complicated because we often justify the use of violence with the authority of religion. We do this when political and economic ends are falsely presented as religious imperatives. We also justify our own violence by pointing to the violence we see in the traditions of the other.

Because violence is such a universal problem common to each of our faiths, it is critical for us to face this inclination in order to heal.

Violence in Judaism

Personal Reflections

My mother tried to keep me from getting a gun. Of course, I was around eight, and the gun in question used caps. Playing cowboys and Indians was much more fun with a "real" gun, instead of the sticks I had been using. Years later, Mom was to share how she failed to keep me from playing "shoot-'em-up," but the violence I knew was mostly make-believe. From adventures on the radio, I constructed the battles in my mind. From television cowboys, I learned how to play that game. My friends and I shadowboxed and pretended to fight each other. Which was fine until I actually got hit.

I was on a group camping trip while in junior high school, and I got in a fight with another boy. I have no idea what the fight was about, but I remember clearly the shock of being hit and falling backward, landing hard on the ground. He punched me in the face! Suddenly, fighting didn't seem much fun at all. That was enough for me. A real fight was nothing like the fights in movies and on TV.

In the ninth grade, I got some further lessons in being on the receiving end of punches. A bully, who seemed to frighten everyone, attacked me because I was Jewish. As I recounted in *Getting to the Heart of Interfaith*, what hurt even more than those punches was the inaction of my friends. I didn't know how to handle the situation, and apparently they didn't either.

Fights were to be avoided at almost any cost. I remember a trip to New York City with my family when I was in high school. We were walking in Manhattan when people emerged from subway stairs, and suddenly a very angry and intoxicated man loomed over my father, accusing him of blocking his way. My dad successfully backed away and avoided a possible confrontation. I realized at that moment a vulnerability I had not known before.

I was taught that Judaism was a religion of peace but that there had always been those who resented us. We were vulnerable because we were a minority, and the Christian majority already had it in for us because their texts implicated us in the death of their Savior.

I was born a month after the attack at Pearl Harbor, when the incredible horrors of the Holocaust were increasingly in the news. Much later we were to learn of the anti-Semitism in the Roosevelt administration that put a damper on our country's response to the mass deportation and murder of European Jewry.

I grew up in a world where violence was perpetrated *against* Jewish people, not *by* them. But when, suddenly, after over two thousand years without political power, the Jews established the

State of Israel in 1948, things changed. We became a player on the world stage, and then we made our own set of political and humanitarian errors. As Louis de Bernières wrote:[1]

> All war is fratricide, and there is therefore an infinite chain of blame that winds its circuitous route back and forth across the path and under the feet of every people and every nation, so that a people who are the victims of one time become the victimizers a generation later, and newly liberated nations resort immediately to the means of their former oppressors. The triple contagions of nationalism, utopianism and religious absolutism effervesce together into an acid that corrodes the moral mettle of a race, and it shamelessly and even proudly performs deeds that it would deem vile if they were done by any other. (256–57)

It is crucial to examine the ways in which this moral corrosion surfaces in all countries. In Israel, the gradual dehumanization of the Palestinians and the delegitimization of their rights reflect the almost universal tendency that Bernières notes above. In many such cases, the drive to acquire power and economic control often masquerade as religion, but the conflict between Israel and Palestinians is not one of religion.

During the Vietnam War years, I became increasingly convinced that war could never actually bring peace. In my first years as a rabbi, I began to counsel young men who wished to obtain status as Jewish conscientious objectors. Because so many Jews had participated in the military, it was more difficult to demonstrate that Judaism supported pacifism. Nevertheless, those of us who worked to help those young men saw many of them receive the status they sought, and go on to perform alternative nonmilitary service to their country. My aversion to war continues. I am convinced that the core teachings of Judaism oppose war as a solution to national problems.

Scriptural and Institutional Support for Violence

It wasn't until rabbinical school that I had to confront the more violent parts of the Torah. The custom at the Reform temple my family attended was to skip over many of those verses during Shabbat readings. But skipping over violent texts did not make them go away, any more than avoiding the news media reports can make the violence in our world disappear.

The fifth and final book of the Torah consists of several of Moses's lengthy teachings to the community of Israel prior to their entry into the Promised Land and expands on the basic spiritual teachings of early Judaism. At the heart of this teaching is the belief in one God, or God's Oneness, and that any competing beliefs and their practices were threats to that central teaching. The punishment for such dangerous beliefs was severe:

> If your brother, your own mother's son, or your son or daughter, or the wife of your bosom, or your closest friend entices you in secret, saying, "Come, let us worship other gods" ... do not give heed to him. Show him no pity or compassion, and do not shield him; but take his life.
>
> *(Deuteronomy 13:7–10)*

Such violent punishment was called for not only against individuals but also against entire cities. The following section is often quoted as a harsh example of violence commanded by God in the Torah:

> If you hear it said, of one of the towns that the LORD your God is giving you to dwell in, that some scoundrels from among you have gone and subverted the inhabitants of their town, saying, "Come let us worship other gods" ... put the inhabitants of that town to the sword and put its cattle to the sword ... burn the town and all its spoil ...
>
> *(Deuteronomy 13:13–17)*

In a later section of the Hebrew Bible, King Saul is faulted for failing to obey God's instruction to utterly destroy all the members and possessions of the tribe of Amalek (1 Samuel 15). Because King Saul did not totally wipe out the community and the property of the Amalekites, he lost the support of the prophet Samuel and of God.

Commands to violence like these were perceived to emanate from God. These are texts Christians used to portray the God of the Hebrew Bible as a punishing and vindictive God, in contrast to the loving and forgiving God of the Christian Scriptures. However, it is important to remember that in order to assert Christian superiority, the many verses supporting love, compassion, and forgiveness in Jewish Scriptures are ignored. Often even Jesus's own teachings, in which he quotes from the Torah of his own tradition, fail to credit that Jewish text. For instance, in far too many texts, "And you shall love the Lord your God ...," and "Love your neighbor as yourself," are credited to Matthew, Mark, and Luke rather than to Deuteronomy (6:5) and Leviticus (19:18).

In pursuit of the spiritual essence of Oneness, Jewish Scriptures deal harshly with polytheistic beliefs and practices. To support the expansion of Christianity, Jewish teachings were often dealt with in similarly harsh ways.

Commentary on Violence

The citations considered with respect to violence in the Torah are, of course, both situationally and historically based. The specific enemies of the path of Oneness practiced pagan rites in direct opposition to the regulations observed by the children of Israel. Their worship often included communal sexual practices forbidden in the Torah. During the biblical period, the essential unit was the tribe, and anything that detracted from tribal integrity was outlawed. Pagan sexual practices, for example, were thought to undermine the basic needs of the developing monotheistic community.

Nevertheless, there is actually no evidence that the commands for total destruction of people and property quoted in the Torah ever took place. The stringent threats of punishment may have inhibited such behavior, which was their intent. The text concerning King Saul, an event occurring many centuries after the events chronicled in the Torah, appears to be one of the historical examples illustrating the actual implementation of such a commandment. And it is certainly not the only text in which violence seems to be supported by the authority of God.

Postbiblical interpretation of the principles of Torah further restricted the use of capital punishment in Jewish tradition. Before the first century of the Common Era, capital punishment in Judaism had been restricted to cases involving murder, and was rendered even more unlikely with the additional rule that the murder needed to be witnessed by no less than two reliable witnesses who warned the perpetrator to desist before the act of killing. That's the actual law, but the reputation of the ancient Jewish legal system was significantly damaged by the way that system is represented in the Christian Scriptures.

In the Christian Scriptures, the Sanhedrin, which was the ruling body of the Jewish community, is portrayed as supporting the death penalty for Jesus (Matthew 26:59, Mark 14:55). The writers of the Christian Scriptures may have been anxious to absolve the Roman leaders of guilt since they were addressing a Greek-speaking audience of the Roman Empire, but their representation of how the Sanhedrin ruled lacks historical accuracy. For one thing, the Sanhedrin could not have met during the festival of Passover, when the drama occurred, nor could the Sanhedrin consider capital cases at night. In addition to these historical discrepancies, the Jews at the time were under Roman rule and did not have that degree of authority over their own legal affairs. No doubt, some Jews opposed Jesus, but he himself and all his followers were Jews.

Until the establishment of the State of Israel in 1948, Jews were not in a position to have legal authority except in religious and ritual matters. It is instructive that in Israel there is no death penalty. The one exception to this ban was the decision to hang

Adolf Eichmann in 1962. Eichmann had been one of the major organizers of the Holocaust, facilitating and managing the logistics of mass deportation of Jews to ghettos and extermination camps in German-occupied Eastern Europe.

THE ISSUE OF OUR OWN VIOLENCE

The most violent creatures on this planet appear to be human beings. We say we want peace, but it's such an elusive goal. We want peace of mind, we want peace at home, and we want peaceful relationships. We want to live in a peaceful country, and we want to have a peaceful world. How could we want something so fervently and still have so little of it?

I believe the violent and violence-provoking passages in scripture reflect the violence that lives in us. The feelings attributed to God in scripture are feelings that we ourselves harbor. In fact, there are many times when the scriptural God seems to be acting more like a human being than like God. Let's find the bad guys and just get rid of them!

When scripture presents a God who demands and judges, who promises and threatens, I believe that we are witnessing a projection of our own ways of thinking rather than a clear representation of a Universal Being. I believe there is a God who demands reconciliation and healing, not violence and killing. Human beings have the freedom to choose, so we have the power to heal or to hurt. Our choices make a world of difference.

The "angry God" portrayed in scripture is the projection of our own fear and our own anger, the "punishing God" reflects our own desire to control, and the "rewarding God" mirrors our own desire for certainty. In each case, the projection is ours. God is so much bigger than we are.

The passages of scripture demonstrating this level of my own being awaken me to what needs healing in me. The more aware I am of the potential for violence within me, the more likely I am to refrain from acting that violence out in my world. The troublesome passages of the Bible offer me support for my spiritual growth as I meet and reintegrate the aspects of my personal identity I would rather not show the world. The universal teachings inspire me to recognize the interconnectedness of all being. *God* is a word I use to point toward that interconnectedness.

Core Teachings and Healing

Like the core teachings in all authentic spiritual traditions, Judaism supports acts of loving-kindness in the world. In the Talmud, the great repository of wisdom and debate completed at the beginning of the sixth century CE, instructions are given regarding the choice of a friend. Notice how people respond when they're angry, the Talmud advises, because anger can lead to destructive behavior. "He who rips his clothing or throws something in his anger, it is as if he worships idols," says the Talmud (Shabbat 105b), indicating that anger itself is not evil, but acts stimulated by anger may be. Violence is action motivated by anger, and it is contrary to the deepest teachings of Jewish tradition.

Rabbinic psychology affirms opposing inclinations within each human being—the *yetzer tov*, or good inclination, and the *yetzer ha-ra*, the evil inclination or the inclination toward self-gratification. Even though we possess an inclination toward self-satisfaction, we can, and must, master it. The essential difference between humans and other animals is our ability to transcend our basic instinctive behaviors in favor of more rational and loving ways of living.

Biblical history testifies to the futility of thinking that a lasting peace can come through violent means. King David was not permitted to construct the central sanctuary, the Temple in Jerusalem, because he had too often been a man of war. His son, Solomon, whose hands were not so stained with blood, was later able to oversee the construction of the Temple that would last for centuries. In *Pirke Avot*, a section of ethical instruction in the Talmud, we find a famous teaching by Hillel, the first-century sage, who said, "Be like the disciples of Aaron, loving peace and pursuing peace" (1:12).

The core teachings of oneness, love, and compassion are never served through violent means. These central tenets provide the balm with which violence can be healed. Although violence is a natural aspect of our being, spiritual teachings of all traditions encourage us to deal with that tendency without acting it out in the world. The simple truth is that the more conscious we are of our potential for violence, the more likely we are to control that impulse when we are threatened. True self-defense, of course, where violence limits violence, may be necessary, but we seek a world in which even that violence is significantly minimized.

While there are many biblical and postbiblical passages promoting peace rather than violence, perhaps the most well-known comes from the book of Isaiah: "They shall beat their swords into plowshares, and their spears into pruning hooks: nation shall not lift up sword against nation, neither shall they learn war anymore" (2:4).

Violence in Christianity
Personal Reflections

One of the tragedies in Christianity is that the Christian church has often been a supporter of wars. Because the teachings of Jesus oppose war, this makes it all the more painful to talk about violence in Christianity.

I was born during World War II and grew up in a culture that acknowledged war as a legitimate way of solving problems. While there was always a small community of dissent, violence was understood to be "natural." Of course, violence *is* natural until the ego is eclipsed by that larger spiritual sensibility that can see other, nonviolent means of solving problems, ways to resist evil, and ways to destroy evil's ability to function.

As a child, my understanding of violence was framed by two realities: my father's decision to become a conscientious objector during World War II, and my obsession with the romantic American West and the image of the cowboy. So, instead of sharing my dad's war stories with my friends, my primary frame of reference was objection to war. At the same time, as early as my sixth birthday, I had pistols and rifles, cowboy hats and boots—all the elements that went into creating the life of that lone romantic hero, the Lone Ranger. I never had any interest in the guns and uniforms of soldiers in World War II. There was nothing romantic about that war for me. It was all too real and because of my dad's decision, I rejected any participation in those activities, which some of my friends enjoyed. But then one night when I was twelve, I was tuning in to *The Lone Ranger* on the radio and I accidentally got a station playing the song "Rock around the Clock." My entire life changed in that moment.

The use of violence in play activities becomes awkward in adolescence when an entirely new set of problems arises. The stresses of adolescence—identity formation, peer pressure, the emerging sense of mortality—bring with them a need to exercise aggression that cannot be satisfied merely by drifting into creating play activities. For me, listening to rock and roll, playing the drums, dancing, learning to play the guitar, and performing in a succession of bands satisfied at least part of the need that violence can also meet. I played music about my teenage angst and about the tendencies toward violence that are so deeply rooted in the ego.

As we get older and as we grow, it is possible to find ways to express aspects of our experience in positive, creative, and imaginative ways, instead of in ways that cause harm and sorrow. In particular, we can express these things through spiritual growth.

Throughout my adolescence, into college, and beyond, I developed an ever-deepening sense that violence was not necessary. I joined the Student Peace Union as a freshman at Macalester College because I was interested in this issue and because I became enamored of the term "nonviolent resistance," which I first heard from Professor Mulford Sibley of the University of Minnesota. Professor Sibley presented an alternative to the more traditional polarity between war and peace, between violence and pacifism. Nonviolent resistance suggested energy and action, even action capable of satisfying that eternal need for aggression. Pete Seeger's music, which was consistent with that theme, resonated with both my passion for music and my passion for peaceful alternatives to solving problems.

No one is exempt from the urge to use violence to solve problems. The need for revenge almost always encompasses the urge to violence. In my life, I have tried to seek nonviolent means of coping with that tendency, ways of bringing about healing, rather than destruction. This search continues in my spiritual life as well.

Scriptural and Institutional Support for Violence

In the Christian Scriptures, there are references to a "sword," references that predict violence, and references that suggest that "judgment" inevitably involves violence as a form of punishment.

In the Gospel of Matthew, we read, "Do not think that I have come to bring peace to the earth; I have not come to bring peace, but a sword" (10:34).

In the Gospel of Luke, we find, "I tell you to all those who have, more will be given; but from those who have nothing even what they have will be taken away. But as for these enemies of mine who did not want me to be king over them—bring them here and slaughter them in my presence" (19:26–27). Later on in that same chapter we read:

> As he came near and saw the city, he wept over it, saying, "If you, even you, had only recognized on this day the things that make for peace! But now they are hidden from your eyes. Indeed, the days will come upon you, when your enemies will set up ramparts around you and surround you, and hem you in on every side. They will crush you to the ground, you and your children within you, and they will not leave within you one stone upon another; because you did not recognize the time of your visitation from God."
>
> *(Luke 19:41–44)*

In Paul's letter to the church at Rome we read, "For the wrath of God is revealed from heaven against all ungodliness and wickedness of those who by their wickedness suppress the truth" (Romans 1:18). But the full wrath of God seems to get its clearest visibility in the passage from the Gospel of Matthew, in which God condemns to eternal suffering those who have not shown charity to those in need: "Then he will say to those at his left hand, 'You that are accursed, depart from me into the eternal fire prepared for the devil and his angels'" (25:41).

During the first couple of hundred years after the death of Jesus, Christians refused to serve in the Roman army. The institution of Christianity—a somewhat ragtag group at that point—was opposed to violence based on the teachings of Jesus. All that changed in 313 CE when Constantine legalized Christianity within the Roman Empire, after which the church was often a strong supporter of violent acts, especially against heretics. Those who did not follow the state-sanctioned religion were often burned at the stake. But the church was also a supporter and sometimes an instigator of organized violence and hatred; for example, during the Crusades and the Inquisition. During Adolf Hitler's reign in Germany (1933–1945), there was an alignment of Christianity and National Socialism voiced by many bishops and pastors. Laypeople were enthralled with the idea that the triumph of Nazism was consistent with the will of God.

It is frightening to look back and see how, over the two thousand years of its history, the Christian church has supported violence and even, in the case of the Crusades, instigated it. In fact, during the Crusades the cross emerged as the symbol not of the unconditional love of God for every human being, but of war, repression, fear, domination, and triumphalism.

The Christian church has not hesitated to use or support the use of force to achieve any goal it deemed worthy. It has even invented a theory of just war, a system of propositions that, when in place, justifies the use of force, violence, and terror. More than anything else, the just-war theory reflects an institutional sensibility devoid of its original substance, the Gospel of Jesus. It ignores the reality that no matter how evil the threat might seem to be, it never goes away when confronted with force, but always reappears later. This is what Walter Wink, professor emeritus of biblical interpretation at Auburn Theological Seminary, so eloquently calls the "myth of redemptive violence"[2] The only way to meet and vanquish an evil force is to *resist* it nonviolently. With the exception of a small group of churches collectively called the "peace churches" (Mennonites, Quakers, Church of the Brethren), and the notable exception of individuals within more mainstream denominations (Martin Luther King, Jr. was ordained in the American Baptist tradition), it has simply been understood that, given the right conditions, the Christian church should support war with a clear sense of divine concurrence.

Commentary on Violence

Jesus's ministry was not calm or relaxed. He brought forth ideas that he knew would cause dissension and possibly violence. In Matthew, we read, "Do not think that I have come to bring peace to the earth; I have not come to bring peace, but a sword" (10:34). A literal reading of this text suggests that Jesus was endorsing violence as a part of his message. But violence is wholly inconsistent with the substance of the Sermon on the Mount. I think this "sword" verse implies that peace does not come easily and reflects the reality that substantive changes in the time of Jesus were brought about by military action. In this verse Jesus is predicting major changes and uses the word *sword,* I think, to show the drama, the depth of what will happen to the world as the Gospel is proclaimed.

In Luke, the verses, "But as for these enemies of mine who did not want me to be king over them—bring them here and slaughter them in my presence" (19:26–27) recall ritual killings from history (see 1 Samuel 15:33). Jesus was concerned about *preventing* future murders while also endorsing practices that would (reminiscent of

Psalm 1) help people to develop lives of positive substance, aware-ness, and working actively for peace. The word *slaughter* might be read as the end of the emptiness within each of us that can always be filled with evil. Violence is prominent among the evil things to which we are vulnerable.

In the prediction previously quoted in Luke 19:41–44, Jesus describes the inevitability of destruction as a consequence of not paying attention to what is going on around us. The last line, "… you did not recognize the time of your visitation from God" sug-gests that revelation from God is constant, but if we are "asleep" we will not be able to connect to it, and the consequence may be vio-lence, suffering, and even death.

Finally, in the familiar story of the Last Judgment, the metaphoric separation of sheep from goats is used as a comparison to the final separation of good people from bad people. But, as in Psalm 1, we are to understand that there are not "good people" and "bad people." There are, instead, people filled with goodness and people devoid of goodness, vulnerable to evil. The value of every human being is the same, but our "contents" do vary. So I think of this story as a way of showing that when healing becomes a reality, the emptiness that is vulnerable to evil will disappear, and we will move ahead as beings filled with the substance of oneness, uncon-ditional love, and compassion. The word *judgment* can mean "to discern," and in this instance, instead of meaning punishment, I think it points to a discernment that finally brings healing.

These are the types of verses that have lent credibility to the idea that, within the Christian faith, violence is not only accept-able, but required. As it will come from God as a punishment to those who have not made the right choices, so people, in their vio-lent actions, will reflect the actions and will of God. But revenge never solves anything. In fact, it only creates additional problems, additional reasons for violence.

We still live in a time when violent wars and punishments are carried out all the time in the name of religion, in the name of democracy, and in the name of the inviolability of the individual in a culture of privilege. Each of us grapples with how to respond to these state-sanctioned forms of violence in our own way. One of the tasks of all religions and spiritual paths is to help us all see how problems can be solved in ways that bring healing rather than more and more destruction and suffering. And one of the tasks of a democracy is to take those peaceful means of dispute resolution into account as it moves forward. In our democracy, the freedom that we hold so dear and which should give us the space and resources to cope with that, has seen many, many failures. The wars we Americans are now waging in Afghanistan and Iraq and our system of criminal justice, incarceration, and capital punishment are among those failures.

Core Teachings and Healing

The inclusive and precious reality of oneness, plus the energy and deep usefulness of unconditional love and compassion, are wholly inconsistent with any sort of violence. But without that inclusive sensibility, there is a vacuum that violence inevitably fills. The core teachings, with their power and value, fill that emptiness with positive energy and the substance of oneness, unconditional love, and compassion.

Violence as a method for solving problems gains its authorization from the *conditions* we place on love. If you are not part of us, if you are not behaving the way we think you should, if you have something that rightfully belongs to us, or if you are doing something that threatens our well-being, we are authorized by those conditions to respond with violence. In other words, you have not met our conditions.

But Jesus teaches us to love our enemies and pray for those who persecute us (Matthew 5:44). I think the only way we can understand the use of the word *love* in that verse is in that sense of love without conditions. There would be no other way to love those we perceive to be enemies.

This is not to say that there will be an end to conflict. As long as we have egos, as individuals and as institutions, there will be conflict. We will always have differing perspectives on experiences and bring different thoughts and feelings to the problems we encounter. And today, those differences often lead to violence, hatred, frustration, and suffering. Each of those consequences appears as an attempt to benefit and protect the ego—the individual ego or the institutional ego. But what if we could learn through our spiritual practices and the preservation of our imaginations to recognize the experience of conflict as an opportunity for growth and creativity? The differences we bring could then be seen as opportunities, even gifts. They could cease to be seen as problems that provoke violence.

In science, conflict is a source of vitality and helps to propel the work of discovery. In religion, conflict could function in the same way, but that would require a consistent conscious awareness of the positive possibilities of differences. Love without conditions is essential to such a way of resolving underlying differences.

Violence in Islam
Personal Reflections

As a native of a country born not once but twice in religious and political violence, I believe I have a few things to say about the use of religion as a disguise and an excuse for the vicious and inexcusable things we humans sometimes do to one another. I was not yet alive when India was partitioned along so-called demographic lines in 1947, but my parents often spoke of the terror that ruled the region as hundreds of thousands of Muslims and Hindus were massacred, and millions more fled their family homes and endured untold hardships to reach safety in their newly assigned countries: India for the Hindus and Pakistan (East and West) for the Muslims. In the end, not all Muslims moved to Pakistan and not all Hindus moved to India, so that, human nature being what it is, there is still mistrust and occasional violence between the two groups even today. Mohandas Gandhi, my personal hero because of his policy of nonviolent, passive resistance against imperialist oppression (known as *Satyagraha*), was appalled at the idea of partitioning India along religious lines. "My whole soul rebels against the idea that Hinduism and Islam represent two antagonistic cultures and doctrines," he said. "To assent to such a doctrine is for me a denial of God."

As it turned out, another partition was in the works, this one setting Muslim against Muslim. Citing a long list of grievances against the central government, leaders in East Pakistan seceded from the Dominion of Pakistan in 1971 and declared independence as the People's Republic of Bangladesh. There followed another horrific war in which hundreds of thousands of people died and ten million became refugees. My brother and I were safely abroad during the turmoil, but my parents and sister were caught in the thick of it. My father, as a Pakistani diplomat, owed his allegiance to the central government, but as the son of a long line of Bengalis, he naturally sided with Bangladesh. This was treason in the eyes of the Pakistani government, and still today I shudder when I think about how narrowly he, along with my mother and sister, escaped almost certain death. By the grace of God they lived to tell the tale of escaping from Pakistan to Bangladesh via Afghanistan and India. I was always amazed at how calmly they told it, with gratitude for those who helped them escape and without rancor toward those who sought to do them harm.

My parents' extraordinary equanimity was caused, I believe, by their deep belief in the Qur'anic message of love and compassion, extended even to one's enemies. The Holy Book enjoins us to repel evil with something far better, so that an enemy becomes an intimate friend. They had deep faith in the universal message of Islam: The all-compassionate God is present in all creation and in every human being, even in those who are not currently manifesting that divinity. This is the spiritual worldview practiced by my

parents and their parents before them, and the view that they tire-
lessly taught their children.

Despite their principled teachings, however, there lurked a
strain of anger in my heart whenever I thought about social injustice, especially when the injustice was directed against my fellow
Muslims. And, here again, I was blessed with a very special
teacher, the Thai envoy to Egypt while my parents were posted
there. This wonderful man, whom I called "Uncle" Sunthorn, was
a devout Buddhist who taught me a powerful lesson about con-
trolling violence in thoughts and words as well as in action.
Listening to me one day as I railed against the hardships and
injustices inflicted on the Palestinians, he complimented me on
my passion for justice but suggested that angry thoughts, when
they fester in the mind, create noxious feelings that give rise to
vengeful fantasies, a volatile combination. When we continue to
feed these feelings and fantasies unmindfully, our hearts become
poisoned, and we are prone to acts of violence. Quoting the
Buddha, he warned me that "We are what we think—everything
that we are arises with our thoughts." Did I want to think myself
into being an angry, volatile young man? Better, he taught, to
negate my angry scenarios by saying "Neti! Neti!" ("Not this! Not
this!") whenever I caught them swirling in my mind. This powerful practice has stood me in good stead for over forty years and
has drastically reduced the energy of violence in my speech and
action, even as I continue to advocate for justice and human rights
for all God's people.

Scriptural and Institutional Support for Violence

Sadly, today many Muslims live in environments of economic depri-
vation and political oppression. Their feelings of anger and powerlessness are exploited by politicians and clerics with an agenda.
Crying "God is great!" some of them have unleashed terror at home
and abroad, falsely invoking the name of God and quoting the
Qur'an for their own violent purposes. People who get their knowl-

edge of Islam from the media reports on Al-Qaeda and other extreme terrorist groups may perhaps be forgiven for thinking the Qur'an is a violent scripture filled with "sword verses" calling for non-Muslim blood, but the truth is quite otherwise. In a volume of more than six thousand verses, less than sixty verses mention fighting or warfare in any context. Such verses are offensive to our twenty-first-century sensibilities, but we simply have to acknowledge that they are there, and interpret them from a higher, more evolved consciousness.

Three Qur'anic verses that speak to intolerance and violence against nonbelievers are:

> But when the forbidden months are past, then fight and slay the pagans wherever ye find them. And seize them, beleaguer them, and lie in wait for them in every stratagem [of war]; but if they repent, and establish regular prayers and practice regular charity, then open the way for them: for God is Oft-forgiving, Most Merciful.
>
> *(9:5)*

> I will instill terror into the hearts of the Unbelievers: Smite ye above their necks and smite all their fingertips off them.
>
> *(8:12)*

> O Prophet! Strive hard against the Unbelievers and the Hypocrites and be firm against them. Their abode is Hell—an evil refuge indeed.
>
> *(9:73)*

These and similar verses are quoted by fundamentalists to justify acts of terror and by non-Muslims to prove that the Qur'an is calling for their blood. In the next section, we shall dig a little further into what the verses really meant at the time they were revealed and explore the ways we can heal the damage their misinterpretation has done to both Muslim and non-Muslim psyches.

Damage has also been done by early classical jurists, who divided the world into the Abode of Islam and the Abode of War and claimed that it was the religious duty of Muslims to "Islamicize" the world, using military force, if necessary. At the time, the religion of Islam was spreading exponentially throughout the Middle East and beyond, and some Muslim leaders relied on their jurists to support war as a means of imperialist expansion that had nothing to do with religion. In modern times, with the political and economic fortunes of Islam drastically reduced, many Islamic extremists take their inspiration from the influential Egyptian scholar Sayyid al Qutb, who stated in his extensive writings that Muslims are mandated to establish Allah's sovereignty on earth. Though he died more than forty years ago (in 1966), his writings still inspire Islamic extremists who call for jihad against the world of nonbelievers.

Commentary on Violence

First, let us consider the "sword verse" of the Qur'an (9:5), which has been so tragically misrepresented by Islamic extremists and misunderstood by fearful Westerners. First, the verse is seriously limited and defined by its historical context. This seventh-century revelation came at a time when the Islamic community in Arabia, a tiny embryonic group in Medina, was miraculously able to survive military assaults from the Quraysh tribe who were overwhelmingly superior in numbers and arms. The community began to consolidate and grow but faced attacks from some pagan tribes who reneged on their treaties. Second, the verse is even more seriously qualified by its textual context. The sword verse also appears in chapter 2, where it is hedged by two Qur'anic commandments. The verse immediately preceding the sword verse in chapter 2 says, "Fight in the cause of God those who fight you, but do not transgress limits; for God loveth not transgressors" (2:190), while the verses immediately following it say, "but if they cease, God is Oft-forgiving, most Merciful…. let there be no hostility…. and know that God is with those who restrain themselves" (2:192–194). Thus the verses that surround the sword verse soften its sharp edges and establish a clear context: The verse refers to defensive fighting, and if the attacker is inclined to peace, the Muslim must cease fighting.

A general principle of Qur'anic interpretation is that if a verse does not seem to support the overall message of the Qur'an or reflect God's divine attributes, we have to dig deeper to reach a more enlightened understanding. So in addition to establishing the contextual limits on this particular revelation—allowing one to kill only in self-defense—it is critical to emphasize that this verse is not about divine permission to kill nonbelievers simply because of their nonbelief or to gain power or control. Such an interpretation would place the verse in direct conflict with the spirit and content of the universal verses in the Qur'an. In an abundance of verses celebrating pluralism and diversity, the Qur'an explains that God could easily have made all of humanity "one single people," but instead created us in beautiful diversity so that we might "vie, then, with one another other in doing good works!" (5:48) and "come to know one another" (49:13). The Holy Book asks rhetorically, "Wilt thou then compel humankind against their will, to believe?" and emphasizes that no matter how much one disapproves of the other's religion, the Muslim is commanded to live and let live: "To you be your Way, and to me mine" (109:6). The Qur'an clearly states that entrance to heaven depends not on religious affiliation but on doing "righteous deeds" (4:124 and 5:69). Except when in mortal danger at the hands of an enemy, Muslims are commanded to repel evil with something better, so that an enemy becomes an intimate friend (41:34).

MAKING PEACE WITH THE SWORD VERSE

Now, how can we make peace with the sword verse? Even if we know that it refers only to self-defense, it is extremely uncomfortable and confusing to read words like, "kill the unbeliever," as a divine revelation. Why would the All-Merciful and All-Powerful God, who has infused every human with divine breath and holds every human heart between divine fingers, instruct anyone to kill? Why would the "Light of the Heavens and Earth" advise a Muslim engaged in battle against his attackers to "smite at their necks" (47:4)? Some of my co-religionists may call me naïve, but when presented with such a puzzlement, I take refuge in Rumi's utterance, "Sell your cleverness and buy bewilderment." What else can one do with a verse like this?

In a continuing attempt to advance my understanding of this difficult verse, I have discussed it with both scholars and students. Some of the scholars, Hindus who are fully conversant with the Qur'an, believe the revelation in question is about God's exhortation to humanity to be courageous and take action in the face of attack by others. Indeed, this line of thought is consistent with another revelation in the Qur'an: "For if God had not enabled people to defend themselves against one another, monasteries and churches and synagogues and mosques—in which God's name is abundantly extolled—would surely have been destroyed" (22:40).

Reinforcing the need for courage when under attack, the scholars cite an epic conversation in the Bhagavad-Gita between Krishna, a Divine Being, and the mortal Prince Arjuna on the eve of engaging in the battle of Kurukshetra. Viewing the multitude of soldiers on the opposing side, the prince laments to Krishna about spilling the blood of "cousins." Krishna berates the prince for using false piety to cover up his fear and lack of courage. Without action, Krishna says, the cosmos would fall out of order.

My students, high school Muslims, suggested that the verse should be interpreted metaphorically. After all, they argued, the Qur'an clearly states that some verses are literal and some are metaphorical (3:7), but it doesn't say which ones are which! To these young, creative minds, the sword verse is about slaying the idols of arrogance and ignorance within ourselves.

Finally, the thirteenth-century sage Rumi claims that any interpretation depends on our level of consciousness and our intention on what we hope to learn. "A bee and wasp drink from the same flower," says Rumi. "One produces nectar and the other, a sting." When I'm troubled by the way the sword verse could be interpreted, I remember that the way of Islam is to produce nectar.

UNDERSTANDING JIHAD

Now, about that terrifying word *jihad:* Thanks to misinformation in the media and misrepresentation by Islamic extremists, many Westerners associate the word *jihad* with "holy war" and suicide bombing. To set the record straight, *jihad* literally means "effort" and refers primarily to the spiritual effort to evolve into the fullness of one's being, to improve relationships with family and neighbors, and to work for justice. The more militant concept of *jihad* that so threatens the Western mind refers only to self-defense when under attack. The idea of *jihad* as "holy war" simply does not exist in the Qur'an, even though this is the prevailing notion not only in the media but also, unfortunately, among some Islamic militants.

What is often overlooked is that for a thousand years after Islam's inception in the seventh century, there was a tradition of vigorous and lively debate among scholars and jurists on contentious issues, including war. The classical jurists' notion of dividing the world into the Abode of Islam and the Abode of War has been hotly contested and refuted by other Islamic jurists. In the fourteenth century, the conservative jurist Ibn Tamiyya argued definitively that such a concept violated the basic Qur'anic principle forbidding "compulsion in religion" (2:256). Even in the twentieth century, when ideological debate among peers and scholars was comparatively lame, the inflammatory views of Sayyid al Qutb were opposed by many of his colleagues and upon his death he was declared a heretic by the scholars of Al-Azhar University, one of the premier universities in the Muslim world.

In recent times, however, the classical doctrine of jihad as holy war has seen a resurgence among militants who chafe against the Muslim experience of colonialism, wars, and occupation. What underlies the resurgence of militancy is not religion but politics. An exhaustive six-year Gallup poll in thirty-five Muslim countries concluded that 7 percent of Muslims are "radicals," and that Islamic militancy is based not on Islamic principles but on political radicalization. In every suicide bombing attack from 1980 to 2004, the primary motive was to overthrow foreign occupation, not to further religious views. Robert Pape, a leading expert on suicide terrorism from the University of Chicago, reports that the vast majority of Islamic suicide bombers come from middle-class backgrounds with a significant level of education. He asserts that the "taproot of suicide terrorism is nationalism." According to Islamic sages, if we focus on religion as the primary cause, we are searching in the branches for what really appears in the roots.

As is so often the case, the remedy for misunderstanding and fear lies in the same texts and traditions that give rise to the problem in the first place. Muhammad proclaimed that the ink of the scholar is more holy than the blood of the martyr, and the word *ilm* (knowledge) is the second-most-repeated word in the Qur'an. It is the sacred task of Muslims and non-Muslims alike to humbly and mindfully examine the scriptural sources of religious violence and allow for a knowledge of the heart to understand and interpret the sacred texts.

The historic "Arab Spring" began in early 2011, when nonviolent, grassroots movements in Tunisia and Egypt astonishingly overthrew autocratic and repressive regimes in a short span of time. This stunning turn of events is reminiscent of how the Prophet Muhammad finally achieved victory in the face of overwhelming odds.

Core Teachings and Healing

It is incumbent on Muslims to know their own history, and here I would remind my sisters and brothers of a watershed treaty between the Muslims and the Quraish tribe in the seventh century. After a series of attacks by the vastly larger forces of the Quraish tribes and their allies, Muhammad's small community in Medina finally achieved peace and freedom of worship not by force of arms but by mysterious spiritual energies unleashed by a treaty of nonviolence known as the Treaty of Hudaibiyah.

It started with a numinous dream in which the Prophet was instructed to travel to Mecca to perform the pilgrimage with his people, with the stipulation that they must make the journey unarmed. His close companion, Umar, protested incredulously that this was like taking "lambs to slaughter," but Muhammad was determined, and a thousand unarmed pilgrims joined the hajj to Mecca. Along the way they narrowly evaded a band of Quraish fighters sent to kill them and managed to reach "safe" territory where fighting was prohibited.

After many harrowing events, including a false report that their envoy, Uthman, had been killed, Muhammad signed a truce with the Quraish. The terms were humiliating to the Muslims: Muhammad would not be allowed to use his title "Messenger of God"; the pilgrims would not be allowed to do the hajj that year; and any defector from the Quraish tribe who chose to go to Medina and become a Muslim without permission of guardians would have to be returned to the Quraish, whereas a defector from Medina who went to Mecca must be allowed to stay there.

Once again, Omar led the protests of the stunned pilgrims, who were dismayed at the terms. "Is not our cause just and the cause of the enemy unjust?" he demanded. "Why should we be humble in our religion?" Nevertheless, the Prophet stood firm in his decision to sign, the protests subsided, and his followers' loyalty prevailed. On the way back from Medina, the would-be hajjis were filled with a strange calm and anticipation. A Qur'anic revelation from that time proclaims, "Verily we have granted thee a manifest victory" (48:1), and a subsequent revelation extols self-restraint: "God sent down His tranquility to His apostle and to the believers and made them stick close to the command of self-restraint" (48:26).

In the ensuing peace, many came to the fold of Islam and the small band began to grow and flourish. Eighteen months later, the Quraish dissolved the treaty. When Muhammad and his followers marched to Mecca, armed this time, they received so much support along the way that their numbers swelled to ten thousand. The

Meccans laid down their arms, and history records that no blood was shed as Muhammad and his followers entered Mecca in triumph. The only act of aggression was the destruction of the idols inside the Kaaba. Two objects in the Kaaba were spared because the Prophet proclaimed them inviolable. These were icons of Mary and Jesus.

According to my father, a history scholar as well as a diplomat, the moment Muhammad signed the Treaty of Hudaibiyah, the community of Muslims was destined to become a world civilization. The treaty signified a commitment to the divine qualities of humility, self-restraint, faith, patience, and peace. These spiritual commitments establish a connection to God, who sends down tranquility into hearts, fills them with "faith upon faith," and rewards them with "manifest victory." The ultimate "manifest victory" is inner and outer peace without engaging in violence.

Concluding Comments

Violent behavior seems to have always been a part of human experience; it appears in all aspects of our lives. So it is no surprise that violence rears its head in our religious traditions as well. As our world grows smaller, we see more clearly how violence anywhere impacts us all, and we need to find ways to resolve human conflict without resorting to force.

In all spiritual traditions, we are offered more peaceful visions of humanity. Recognizing our violent tendencies, we can consciously respond more lovingly toward others. Even in situations of great conflict, spirituality provides peaceful alternatives. One can only get to true peace peacefully.

Sharing Our Stories

Sometimes when we speak it is as if there is an elephant in the room. That elephant is the distress over the situation between Israelis and Palestinians. We can't count the number of conversations we ourselves continue to have about this sensitive and painful issue, nor can we count the number of times it has been raised during the Q&A sessions of our talks.

One of the most difficult of such times for Rabbi Ted occurred when we spoke with a group of high school students in Seattle. Among them were three exchange students, two Palestinians and one from Lebanon. Ted knew that a discussion of politics would not be appropriate after their descriptions of the terrors they had lived through. It was not a time to talk about the Israeli losses to suicide bombers. It was simply a time to listen and to empathize with their anguish.

The most volatile moment we have experienced together also took place at one of our talks in the Northwest. Among those in the audience was an American man who, as part of a group supporting the Palestinians, had made several recent trips to Gaza. We responded as best we could to his questions, but he was swift to approach Ted following our presentation.

"I don't think you answered my questions, Rabbi," the man began.

"I'm sorry," Ted said, and extended his hand. "I'm Ted. What's your name?" The man did not take his hand.

"My name used to be Paul, but I changed it to Ismael because I identify with the horrible plight of the Palestinian people." He took a step closer to Ted. "A plight created by you Jews."

"I know that there is suffering on both sides," Ted began, but before he could say anything more, he was shouted down.

"The Israelis have all the power. There is no suffering there. *They* are the cause of the suffering." The man's face was flushed. "They took the land," he yelled, "with help from Roosevelt and the Jewish lobby in America. They forced people from their homes. *They* are the oppressors. There is no question about that." His voice was getting louder and louder. He had long since attracted the nervous attention of those still in the room.

Jamal stepped between Ted and Ismael, and with his usual welcoming demeanor and calm voice, he said, "I know that this is a terrible situation, but we need to be able to talk about it without shouting at each other."

But Ismael couldn't feel that. He moved closer to Jamal and pushed him in the chest. "And you, you call yourself an imam, but you're even worse than him. You're a traitor to your people. You're a traitor to be friends with this rabbi!" His hands came up to push again, and suddenly Pastor Don, who is considerably taller than Jamal and Ted, stepped in.

We'd like to ask you to take a breath at this point, because we need to tell you that nothing physical erupted as a result of this confrontation. But we suspect that the story caught your attention, didn't it? And this is one of the problems with violence. It's newsworthy. It compels us to take notice. We might like to be nonviolent people, yet we are inexorably drawn to depictions of violence.

During the early years of our work together, a producer from National Public Radio contacted Rabbi Ted to talk about his activities with Imam Jamal and Pastor Don. During the conversation, she asked Ted how he and Jamal stopped fighting with each other. Ted was silent for a moment, then said, "Well, actually, we never fought. It just didn't happen that way."

And that was the end of the conversation. The producer politely thanked him for his time and concluded the conversation. For a long time, it seemed that we were too peaceful for press coverage. Maybe, we joked, people would be more willing to listen to our message of peace if we staged some kind of public fight so that we could then publicly reconcile.

Violence is the eruption of anger. It is most often thought of as physical, but violence can also be emotional and mental. As a culture, we are becoming more aware of the violence that comprises emotional and mental abuse and often goes unrecognized until too much damage has been done. Still, the violence of the bully gets the most attention, and many programs have been instituted to decrease the victimization of others by such bullies.

The most effective program we know about comes from the Netherlands, where researchers noted that there are three parties to the drama: the bully, the victim, and the witnesses. They realized that those who had the power to change the situation were the witnesses who remain silent and uninvolved during such bullying episodes. Rather than just telling victims to stand up for themselves, they began training the bystanders to take immediate action when they saw bullying behavior.

This is a valuable lesson for all of us, since most of us are not involved in perpetrating violence. We need to find ways to curb our appetite for the dramatic violence that spills over into the real world. We need to grow in awareness so that we are no longer manipulated by the promise of violence depicted in our media. It's up to us. We are the witnesses.

Questions for Discussion

- When news of violence against those of your group or any other group angers you, what is your initial reaction? Do you think about retaliation or revenge? How can you soften the sharp edges of your reactions so that you can think critically and take proper action?

- You have seen that there are many instances of violent behavior supported by our religious traditions. At the same time, there are teachings promoting more peaceful resolution of conflict. Do you think that all conflicts can be resolved peacefully? Is war ever justified? Do you believe that violence leads to more violence?

- Have you ever been a victim of violence? Have you ever been violent to others? What was the effect of the violence you experienced? Looking back, are there other reactions that might have worked better?

Spiritual Practices

From Jewish Tradition

Meditate on the Hebrew word *shalom*, or the English, *peace*. The Hebrew root of *shalom* means "to make whole," teaching that true peace always flows from our essential wholeness. Focusing on *shalom* or *peace* helps open us to inner peace and center our awareness, even in the midst of conflict.

From Christian Tradition

"Blessed are the peacemakers" (Matthew 5:9). The whole text is "Blessed are the peacemakers for they shall be called the children of God," but use the first phrase for your meditation. Jesus taught a path of peace. Meditate on this phrase to create deeper inner support for nonviolent action in the world.

From Islamic Tradition

Meditate on the insight of Sufi masters who teach: "In dealing with the other, do what is right. Protect yourself. Don't allow yourself to be abused. But please do not leave the other person's being out of your heart." We are asked to make a distinction between behavior and being. A person's behavior might be evil, but a person's being is sacred and inviolable. It is filled with Christ Nature, Buddha Nature, Elohim Nature, Allah Nature, Krishna Nature. Just keeping this discernment in mind in our speech and actions has the power to shift heaven and earth.

Chapter Three

Inequality of Men and Women

The Patriarchal Stranglehold on Power

E ach of our Abrahamic traditions evolved within patriarchal cultures, so the inequality of power held by men and women is not surprising. The male power structure has claimed an exclusive right to their power and control.

We recently saw a bumper sticker that proclaimed: "Feminism is the radical idea that women are people." It is startling to be reminded of just how unequal the traditional power structure has been, and how recent the advancements toward equality. We do not yet live in a world in which this equality has been fully achieved, but the journey toward true equality can be aided by recognizing the religious foundations not only of inequality but of possibilities for healing.

Inequality of Men and Women in Judaism
Personal Reflections

When Pastor Don, Imam Jamal, and I present our programs in various cities across the country, we are often aware that one of us should have been a woman. It feels awkward now for three men to be talking, in turn, about the inequality of men and women. This is odd, since I do not feel odd talking about exclusivity, even though I try not to be exclusive; I am fine talking about violence as a nonviolent person; and it's okay to be talking about homosexuality as a straight person. What is it about this particular topic that makes me uneasy? I suspect that I am embarrassed by some of the patriarchal gestalt that characterized my childhood and formative years. Looking back, I realize that there were times when I simply took for granted that the man's job opportunities were primary. And I am also uncomfortable realizing the degree to which I had been blind (and wonder whether that blindness persists) to the inequalities of the sexes. Perhaps the best I can do is share the paradoxes with which I grew up.

Even though I know that men held most of the power in the world in which I was raised, as a child it sometimes seemed quite the opposite. Women ruled the house and the children. In the early sitcoms, like *The Adventures of Ozzie and Harriet,* the father was often a comic character who had precious little grasp of what was going on, while the wife held the awareness and the power to act. The man needed the woman to help him look good and keep from making a fool of himself.

Beyond the sitcoms and my early home experience, it was clear that I lived in a world where men garnered far more respect than women. Both my parents were professionals, my father a CPA and an attorney, and my mother a clinical social worker. Both worked full time before I was born, yet it took a long time for me to recognize that my mother was a professional just like my father. After all, she stayed home with my sister and me and didn't return to work until we were almost in high school. She took care of the house, and Dad earned the money. On those special occasions when Dad took my sister, Barbara, and me to his office, we entered an entirely different world, where he was clearly the boss, where his secretary seemed happy to work for him. He had the freedom to do as he pleased while Mom took care of us kids, the house, the meals, the shopping, and the doctor and dentist appointments. Even after my mother returned to work, she was the one to stay home with us if we were ill.

When I went to rabbinical school, there were no ordained women rabbis, but the woman who would become the first American female rabbi was already beginning her rabbinic program. The whole idea of a woman rabbi elicited a kind of schizophrenic reaction from me. On the one hand, it was obvious that women should have the same opportunities as men. They were at least equal in academic and counseling abilities. But I wondered whether congregations would really accept a woman as their rabbi. Wasn't the rabbi a father figure rather than a mother figure? Certainly, there were periods of adjustment as women began to take congregational positions, but soon the rabbinic seminaries had a large percentage of women students, and there are now well over five hundred women rabbis in the Reform Jewish movement alone.

Although we have come a long way, the reality is that gender inequality still abounds in our culture and in the world. Women almost always earn less than their male counterparts, even when they are doing the same work. There are gender biases built into the languages we speak; in Hebrew and many other languages, the masculine plural is used even when the crowd is mixed. Some levels of inequality are very deeply embedded in our consciousness.

Scriptural and Institutional Support for the Inequality of Men and Women

Gender imbalance certainly characterizes the Tanach, the Jewish Scriptures. The Hebrew Bible clearly portrays a patriarchal system that had supplanted an earlier matriarchal society. The God of the Hebrew Bible is a male figure, even though that God is imbued with many qualities usually thought of as feminine, like compassion and love. Oftentimes, the more masculine, warrior-like qualities of command and control, of reward and punishment, are paramount. In biblical patriarchal times, the male tribal leaders controlled the women in their tribe. Women were subservient, only inheriting from their fathers if there were no male heirs anywhere in the family system (but at least in such a situation they were able to inherit).

Perhaps most significantly, all the religious leaders were male. Only men could be priests, all the major prophets were male, and there were no ruling queens in the ancient Israelite kingdom. In the patriarchal system, women did not have the same rights as men and were often treated as property rather than as persons.

It is clear right from the beginning of Genesis that men were designed to be more powerful than women. The man was the first created, and he shares masculine qualities with his Creator. The woman was later taken from the man, a lesser creature who was to be subservient to the rule of her husband:

> And to the woman He said, "I will make most severe your pangs in childbearing; in pain shall you bear children. Yet your urge shall be for your husband, and he shall rule over you."
>
> *(Genesis 3:16)*

This verse has sometimes been cited as justification for abusive behavior toward women. It is very difficult to forge an egalitarian approach to the sexes in the face of a verse like this.

One of the ways the difference in power and authority is reflected in the Hebrew Bible regards the ability to choose one's own way to make choices in life. This is illustrated in the making of vows. Unlike men, women are not free to make vows and promises to God:

> If a woman makes a vow to the LORD or assumes an obliga-tion while still in her father's household ... [and] if her father restrains her on the day he finds out, none of her vows or self-imposed obligations shall stand ...
>
> *(Numbers 30:4–6)*

In the Bible, a woman's power of self-determination continues to be limited after marriage by her husband, who then carries the same ability to nullify her vows: "Every vow and every sworn obligation of self-denial may be upheld by her husband or annulled by her husband" (Numbers 30:14). In matters of divorce, this inequality is consistent. Divorce is allowed in biblical times, but only the man can initiate it:

> [If] a man takes a wife and possesses her, [and] she fails to please him because he finds something obnoxious about her, and [then] he [can] write her a bill of divorcement, hand it to her, and send her away from his house.
>
> *(Deuteronomy 24:1)*

In ancient times, it was assumed that the ability to have children, and the sex of the children, both depended on the woman. Therefore, should a woman fail to bear children, or fail to provide her husband with a male heir, divorce was possible so that the husband could find a proper wife.

Commentary on the Inequality of Men and Women

Many of the cultural issues grounded in the Bible continued to be practiced through many generations of Jewish experience. For example, in Orthodox Judaism, women still cannot initiate the divorce process, a difficulty that has sometimes created great anguish. A couple might be separated, their marriage essentially over, but if the husband does not grant his wife a religious divorce, the woman is unable to marry again within Orthodox or even Conservative Jewish tradition.

On the other hand, there have been great positive changes in the rights of women to divorce within all branches of Judaism. Within Conservative Judaism and some Modern Orthodox communities, prospective husbands are asked to sign a declaration that, should the woman ever desire a religious divorce he pledges to provide it. This document is typically signed along with the traditional marriage agreement at wedding ceremonies. In the more liberal branches of Judaism, no religious divorce is necessary, since a secular divorce is considered sufficient.

Jewish women have always been among the most vocal feminists. Betty Friedan, whose 1963 book, *The Feminine Mystique*, sparked the entire feminist movement, was Jewish, as were many other feminist leaders. And, of course, women finally entered the active rabbinate in 1972. (Although the first woman to be ordained a rabbi, Regina Jonas, was ordained in Germany in 1935, it wasn't until 1972 that the Hebrew Union College–Jewish Institute of Religion ordained the first American woman rabbi, Sally J. Priesand, and welcomed female students into its rabbinic program.) There are now women rabbis serving congregations in every branch of Judaism except Orthodoxy. Even there, however, women have increasingly led prayer circles of their own, and there are well-recognized Orthodox women teachers of Torah in Israel, whose students include some of the ranking Orthodox rabbis.

ANOTHER LOOK AT THE BIBLE

There is no arguing that the world of the Hebrew Bible is a patriarchal system, with a culture ruled by men. Yet every time I read the narratives of the earliest patriarchs, I am struck by the significant impact their wives made.

As we see in the beginning of Genesis 16, Sarah, the favored wife of Abraham, has trouble conceiving a child. This is a motif repeated often in the Hebrew Bible, and indicates not only the importance of the woman involved, but also the significance of her children. Sarah instructs her husband, Abraham, to take her handmaiden, Hagar, and have a child with her. Some years after Ishmael is born from that union, Sarah becomes pregnant, with divine blessing, and Isaac is born. Sarah then insists that Isaac be the prominent son and instructs Abraham to release Hagar and Ishmael into the wilderness. Strikingly, Sarah is the significant decision maker in the family system. Hers is hardly the image of the subservient wife.

In the next generation, the influence of Isaac's wife, Rebecca, is even more pronounced. In Genesis 27, it is Rebecca who chooses Jacob, and not his firstborn twin brother, Esau, as the one to continue the tribal lineage. It is Rebecca who designs the ruse that results in her nearly blind husband, Isaac, giving the blessing of the firstborn to Jacob, rather than to Esau. It is Rebecca who then urges Jacob to flee from the anger of his brother.

Behind the apparent subservience of the matriarchs is another kind of legitimate power. This is the same power that so many centuries later would be reflected in the episodic comedy of early television. And this is the same power that is seen in what appears to be relatively circumscribed roles of Modern Orthodox and ultra-Orthodox women. My own experience with an ultra-Orthodox part of my family in Safed, Israel, has taught me that roles for women that I might find limiting can be freely and joyfully chosen. Although these women have numerous children and take on the vast majority of housework and childrearing while their husbands spend their days learning holy texts, the wives often feel that their lifestyle is as much a chosen option as their husbands'. In many such relationships, where the husbands spend most of their time studying, the wives help support the family financially and are able to pursue a wide range of career options.

Core Teachings and Healing

Because there are too many women who do not experience the freedom to choose their own way in the world, the quest for equality between the sexes is not complete. Still, it is important to note that the Bible does promote such equality from the very beginning of time. Consider the first time people are mentioned in the Bible: "And God created man in His image, in the image of God He created him; male and female He created them. God blessed them" (Genesis 1:27–28). In this first chapter of Genesis, men and women are created equal. Each is an equal being created in the divine image. Even though the male pronoun is used for God, that does not imply that God is male. On the contrary, God is seen as beyond gender, but reflecting both male and female characteristics. Because the Hebrew language has no neuter forms, everything is either male or female, whether animate or inanimate. So the male pronoun and verb forms are used for God without actually signifying the masculinity of divinity.

Although most of the fifty-five prophets in scripture are men, there are seven women included in the list. Among the judges, Deborah was a major figure during the period prior to the monarchy. And Miriam, the sister of Moses and Aaron, is one of the primary characters in the wilderness saga. Tradition has it that it was because of Miriam's presence that wells of water were found to sustain the community during those long years of wandering.

The core teachings of oneness, love, and compassion require us to support true equality for men and women. But men need to listen to the experience of the women to determine the degree of equality they experience, and women need to share experiences of inequality with the men in their lives. If we are to truly awaken more fully to our shared humanity and our common divinity, we must share more honestly and listen more compassionately. Being more aware of the possibilities of inequality may well be the first step toward healing.

Inequality of Men and Women in Christianity
Personal Reflections

Although I grew up with parents whose roles were traditionally gendered, I was taught to be open to considering alternatives. When I was young, my mother seemed to be the very model of the sort of housewife portrayed in magazine and television commercials. But she also taught piano lessons in our home after school, and so she departed slightly from the commercial image. When my dad came home, he either did chores or sat and read the paper (sometimes he smoked his pipe) while my mother made dinner.

After dinner, my dad read the paper some more while my mother washed the dishes. My dad did his chores later in the evening or on the weekends. So, initially, I learned that there were activities common to men and activities common to women. When I was in middle school, my mother started to teach English. My mother's profession shifted the roles in our house to some extent, and at that point my dad began to help with the dishes. I observed flexibility in these role-defining activities.

When I was married in 1966, I think it was that flexibility that helped to define the way my wife and I divided the domestic chores. And since we were both teaching when we started our married life in Sidon, Lebanon, there was no question that we would need to divide the chores. I did the cleaning and Judy cooked. We each felt it would be important to share in the work of our life together.

This understanding became very important to me as a senior seminarian, when I was fortunate to receive a field education position working for the Presbyterian Council on Theological Seminaries in New York. My position was as a liaison between the Council and the newly created Presbyterian Task Force on Women and the Church. My job was to persuade several seminary professors to write position papers on the topic of women and the church, and to participate in meetings of the Task Force (which included Maggie Kuhn of the Gray Panthers in Philadelphia). The women and men of the Task Force taught me much about the substance of Betty Friedan's book, *The Feminine Mystique,* and gave me an initial picture of the inequality between men and women in the life of the Christian church since the time of the Emperor Constantine.

I learned about inclusive language, began to try to understand what it would be like to be a woman who wished to fill a professional role in the church, and generally came to a deeper understanding of the history of the inequality of men and women. When I graduated from the seminary in 1970, there were four women in my class of 104. By the time I stopped working at the seminary ten years later, about half of each class were women. During that ten-year period, the entire culture of Princeton Seminary changed. When I was a student, there was one woman on the faculty. By 1980, there were many women on the faculty, a center for women's studies had been established, and professors who had been in the habit of greeting their classes with "Good morning, men" had changed their vocabulary.

I experienced that particular ten-year transition as associate director of field education. It was during that time that we encountered our first case of alleged sexual harassment of a female student working in a church supervised by a male pastor. I also realized that the rule prohibiting part-time students from receiving financial support for certain field education assignments was unfair, since many of those part-time students were women seeking a second career (or a first career outside the home at midlife).

While working at the seminary, I was to recall many times the words I had heard from Maggie Kuhn on that Task Force on Women: "All human and civil rights should be available to all people regardless of race or social standing—men and women, young and old *period!*" Her forthrightness stayed with me, helping to shape my entire ministry. More than anything else, I learned over time that some balance between a masculine and a feminine way of understanding experience would be needed to overcome the unrelieved masculinity that had shaped Western culture until then. Today, more than forty years later, such a balance is critical to interfaith dialogue and collaboration. Boundaries must be crossed and trust must be developed in order for genuine spirituality to have a lasting, positive effect on the world.

Scriptural and Institutional Support for the Inequality of Men and Women

One of the best-known verses from the letter to the church at Ephesus is this: "Wives be subject to your husbands" (Ephesians 5:22). Many other verses in the Christian Scriptures reflect this sense, including 1 Corinthians: "But I want you to understand that Christ is the head of every man, and the husband is the head of his wife, and God is the head of Christ" (11:3). Later on in that same chapter we read, "Neither was man created for the sake of women, but woman for the sake of man" (1 Corinthians 3:8–9).

In 1 Timothy, we also read:

> Let a woman learn in silence with full submission. I permit no woman to teach or to have authority over a man, she is to keep silent. For Adam was formed first, then Eve; and Adam was not deceived, but the woman was deceived and became a transgressor. Yet she will be saved through child-bearing, provided they continue in faith and love and holiness, with modesty.
>
> *(2:11–15)*

Finally, in 1 Peter, "Husbands, in the same way, show consideration for your wives in your life together, paying honor to the woman as the weaker sex ..." (3:7). Notice that all these references are from the letters following the Gospels. Nothing in Jesus's teachings suggests weakness or inferiority in women. On the contrary, he honors their full humanity. For example, in the story of Mary and Martha (Luke 10:38–42), Jesus makes it clear that women should not be relegated to a life where thoughtfulness plays no role. Mary's attention to Jesus's teachings reflects what only men would have been permitted to do. And in the story of the anointing of Jesus at Bethany (Mark 14:3–9), an act of compassion attributed to a woman is raised to the level of a teaching moment. The practice of the subjugation of women would rarely have permitted a teaching story to have a woman as a central character.

While there is evidence that the early church genuinely tried to honor the integrity and status of women equally with men (Acts 5:14 and 8:12), the gradual development of a leadership hierarchy coincided with the gradual exclusion of women from positions of power in the church. It is easy to see how the culture of Christianity morphed into patterns that more clearly reflected the cultures in which Christians were living. So it is not surprising that the vast majority of leaders of the early and medieval church taught that women were inferior to men. In his great work, *Summa Theologica*,[1] Thomas Aquinas said:

> As regards the individual nature, woman is defective and misbegotten, for the active force in the male seed tends to the production of a perfect likeness in the masculine sex; while the production of woman comes from defect in the active force or from some material indisposition, or even from some external influence; such as that of a south wind, which is moist, as the Philosopher observes (*De Generatione Animalium* [On the Generation of Animals], Iv. 2). On the other hand, as regards human nature in general, woman is not misbegotten, but is included in nature's intention as directed to work of generation. Now the general intention of nature depends on God, Who is the universal Author of nature. Therefore, in producing nature, God formed not only the male but also the female.

Because the institution of the church was so clear about the inferiority of women, during the medieval period and up until the nineteenth century, there were no women in positions of ordained pastoral leadership. Antoinette Brown was the first woman to be ordained in a mainline denomination in America (in a Congregational church in New Hampshire in 1853). After the Civil War, many other ordinations followed, but it was not until the mid-twentieth century that Presbyterians voted to ordain women both as elders and as ministers. Today there are still Protestant churches that bar women from leadership, and in the Orthodox churches and the Roman Catholic Church it is still impossible for a woman to become a priest.

Commentary on the Inequality of Men and Women

Although the verse from Ephesians is not surprising, given the context in which it was written, the idea that women are to "be subject to" men helped to create the historic Christian support for the primary role of men in society. This was a step back from how Jesus himself honored the role of women.

It was not until the nineteenth century in America that women began to question their unequal status publicly. The important gathering at the home of Elizabeth Cady Stanton in Seneca Falls, New York, in 1848 produced the document, "Seneca Falls Declaration of Rights and Sentiments." Many would argue that the women's suffrage movement was, in fact, a Christian movement—that is, a movement rooted in the substance of Jesus's teachings. The movement for women's suffrage finally realized its goal with the ratification in the early twentieth century of the Nineteenth Amendment, granting women the right to vote. The movement that started in 1848 became, over a period of over one hundred years, the women's liberation movement. Starting with the fight for the right to vote, this movement continued to evolve and sharpen its focus on inequality until it blossomed into the full-fledged feminist movement of the 1960s.

While Betty Friedan's *Feminine Mystique* paved the way for the feminist movement, Rachel Carson launched the environmental movement with her book, *Silent Spring*, imparting an essential feminine sensibility to the topic. Those two books not only awakened a culture to the issue of inequality between the sexes, but they also helped to recall the advocacy work that had been going on among and for women since that moment in 1848.

A synergy of factors—including the feminist movement, the civil rights movement, and the environmental movement—gave birth within the Christian church to a change of heart concerning the role of women in the church. Women and men, like those whom I met on the Presbyterian Task Force on Women and the Church in 1969, started to work hard for equal rights for women in positions of leadership in the church. The first such positions were directors of religious education.

When the first Sunday School was started in Gloucester, England, in 1780, the clergy (all men) did not wish to be a part of it. In the nineteenth century as the movement grew into the International Sunday School Movement, it was entirely lay-led, with hardly any support from the clergy. That movement was incorporated into the National Council of Churches in the twentieth century, and it was then that women began to be trained as directors of religious education. Some might say that that was a step forward, because it gave women a place of leadership in the church hierarchy. But others would say that it was simply a way to marginalize women, because the male clergy were still not interested in sharing their knowledge of the faith.

As women advanced in their roles as education directors, the Presbyterian Task Force on Women and the Church made it clear that women were also as capable as men of pursuing ordained leadership (the Presbyterian Church had been ordaining women since the mid-1950s but by 1969, there were still very few ordained women). One could say that Christian people, having been awakened by secular movements, were now able to see that equal status for men and women was, and is, fundamentally in keeping with the message of Jesus.

Core Teachings and Healing

Oneness, unconditional love, and compassion—together and separately—suggest support for the essential dignity and self-worth of all people, since we are all a part of the One. Nothing in our core teachings would support a theological, psychological, or spiritual exclusion of women from any activity in life. Only a cultural fear, generated by the concerns of the ego, would undergird such exclusion.

Patriarchy—the sense that men are needed to guide the progress of the world—would be threatened by a world where equal rights are granted to women, a world in which a better balance of masculine and feminine energies would contribute to essential fairness and justice. That balance of masculine and feminine energies would result in a more just world for all people and a greater mental and spiritual equanimity for everyone.

Unconditional love actually depends on that balance. For example, if I say, "There is nothing you can do to make me stop loving you," I may feel that I am giving away a part of my self, my authority, my power. But Jesus taught us that in offering unconditional love, quite the opposite is true. For the first time, we live into the essential wholeness of our beings when we offer unconditional love. We become full, whole, embracing that balance of masculinity and femininity without which we are incomplete, and without which we seek to complete ourselves in ways that cause pain and suffering for other people. Unconditional love is essential as a counterweight to the masculine fear of being weak and losing a part of the self in loving without conditions.

The movement toward full equality for women and men is a movement that brings justice to the lives of women. It also brings a sense of being complete that could have an impact on all the places where we need healing.

Inequality of Men and Women in Islam
Personal Reflections

By the grace of God, I was blessed with parents whose marriage exemplified the beauty of the Qur'anic injunction to "live with them on a footing of kindness and equity" (4:19). Though the verse was revealed to instruct men to love and honor their wives, both of my parents took it to heart in their treatment of each other. Growing up under their tutelage, I heard repeatedly that the Qur'an and the Prophet Muhammad honored women to a degree unheard of in the brutal time and place that gave rise to the new religion of Islam. Declaring that paradise lies at the feet of one's mother, the Prophet forbade slander against women and urged his followers to obey the Qur'anic verses granting women the right to divorce and to own and inherit property—unprecedented rights that the men of seventh-century Arabia were not prepared to grant. To appreciate how truly radical this was, consider that it was happening during the Dark Ages, and that the status of women in the West by and large did not begin to improve until the late nineteenth century.

Sadly, and often tragically, the honor accorded to women in the Qur'an has not translated into reality on the ground. My parents' diplomatic career took us to many Islamic countries, and I saw firsthand the unequal status of women, especially in rural villages. Millions of Muslim women are relegated to a life of illiteracy and economic dependence on their husbands. Severely restricted in their ability to leave the home or participate in public life, they are dominated by their husbands and exist only to serve the males in their households and teach their daughters to do the same. My parents often remarked on the appalling status of women in the Islamic countries we visited, but they also observed that female inequality is rooted not in religion but in the entrenched traditions of patriarchal societies that existed long before Islam arrived. Once tribal and cultural traditions take root, no matter how inequitable, it takes considerable time and sustained effort to uproot them.

In my early teens, I witnessed an incident in Mecca that brought me face-to-face with the disrespect women must put up with, even in the birthplace of Islam. One evening, as my mother and I were praying in the grand mosque, we were accosted by a burly and belligerent member of the religious police, who waved a stick and wagged his finger while berating my mother for having a part of her shoulder exposed. (My mother usually wore the traditional Bangladeshi outfit of a sari with a short-sleeved blouse and a lovely long shawl over one shoulder—very beautiful and absolutely modest.) My brother and I were her male "escorts" that evening. We were filled with impotent rage over our inability to protect her honor in the face of that overbearing bully. My mother, however, defended herself with her calm but forceful manner, and the policeman retreated. The moment passed, but not before I had absorbed a lasting lesson about the indignity and discrimination Muslim women suffer at the hands of dominant men.

Scriptural and Institutional Support for the Inequality of Men and Women

Although the majority of Qur'anic verses are neutral in regard to gender rights, and some are specifically favorable to women, there are a few verses that have caused considerable controversy and damage to the dignity and welfare of Muslim women. Chief among these is the infamous verse about beating a troublesome wife (4:34). Translations abound, including the following:

> As for those women whose defiance you have cause to fear, admonish them and keep them apart from your beds, and beat them.[2]

> As to those women on whose part ye fear disloyalty and ill-conduct, admonish them [first], [next], refuse to share their beds, [and last] beat them [lightly].[3]

> As for those women [on whose part] you apprehend disobedience and bad behavior, you may admonish them [first lovingly] and [then] refuse to share their beds with them and [as a last resort] punish them [mildly].[4]

The Arabic language of the Qur'an lends itself to a variety of translations, not to mention interpretations, ranging from bare-bones Arabic-to-English renditions to a more nuanced presentation of what an Arabic word or phrase is meant to convey. There is a similar range from stark to nuanced in translations of a verse that seems to suggest that wives are at the disposal of their husbands for sexual pleasure: "Your wives are as a tilth unto you; so approach your tilth when or how ye will" (2:223).

In addition to these verses, there are some institutional practices that suggest or support patriarchal bias, oppression, and violence against women, namely: male polygamy, segregation of women in mosques, stoning of women convicted of adultery, and genital mutilation. And, finally, in our list of factors that have contributed to the mistreatment of women in Islam, let us not forget the innumerable misogynistic ahadith in which Muhammad is supposed to have said, "Men perish when they obey women," "But for women, man would have entered Paradise," and similar scornful remarks.

Commentary on the Inequality of Men and Women

Qur'anic interpretation requires patience, reflection, and knowledge of the Arabic language. Arabic root words can have a number of different meanings, as is clear from the various translations just cited, and the choice of meaning often depends on who is doing the interpreting. Take the word *nushuz,* which most men would interpret as "domestic defiance," but which female scholars interpret as "open, public rebellion against repression by one's husband." So does the Qur'an recommend punishment for marital spats, or only for public scenes in which the woman deserts or humiliates her husband because she is tired of being confined to private seclusion and ill treatment? And what is that punishment to be?

The root word *daraba* is almost always interpreted by men as "beat," but women point out that the word is used several times in the Qur'an in contexts that do not suggest beating but could mean either "go away from" or "turn away from." The Qur'an describes marriage as a union of mutual "love and mercy," in which man and woman are "garments" and "protectors" of each other: "It is He who has created you all out of one soul, and out of it brought into being a mate so that man might incline with love towards woman" (7:189). Is this the same Holy Book that would advise men to beat their God-given wives?

Even if there were a divine sanction to beat disobedient or disloyal women, albeit "lightly" or "symbolically," it would be unacceptable in this day and age. A symbolic beating, such as "a tap that leaves no mark," may have been considered progressive in the seventh century, when men killed women on the slightest pretext, but today we know it is offensive, inhumane, and illegal. In this matter, we have to assume that the Qur'an was taking a gradualist approach, as it did for slavery, which was not forbidden but was strongly discouraged.

The Prophet did not take such a gradualist approach. Contrary to those spurious ahadith in which he supposedly scorned women, historical accounts relate that he commanded his followers not to harm their wives. "Never beat God's handmaiden," he said.[5] When they resisted—even his close companion, the gentle Abu Bakr, insisted on the right to discipline his wives—Muhammad exclaimed, "What! Does one of you hit his wife and then attempt to embrace her? Only the worst of you will have recourse to such methods!"[6]

Regarding the verse about wives being their husband's "tilth," the true meaning emerges from the textual context. For desert Arabs, an arable and fertile piece of land is sacred and precious. The use of the word *tilth* in this verse is a metaphor that is meant to remind men how sacred their wives are and how precious is their potential for new life. The same verse continues with an admonition to "provide something for your souls and remain conscious of God," which inspired the Qur'an translator-commentator Muhammad Asad to write in a footnote, "A spiritual relationship is postulated as the indispensable basis of sexual relations."[7]

We come now to some of the institutional practices that are clearly harmful to women. First is the issue of polygamy, which the Qur'an permits but only under very special circumstances. The verse permitting a man to take up to four wives (4:3) arose in the context of an urgent need to protect abandoned orphans and widows in times of war. But even in those circumstances, the Qur'an allows multiple marriages only if the husband is able to distribute his affection equally between his wives. The Holy Book cautions, "And it will not be within your power to treat your wives with equal fairness, however much you may desire it" (4:129), effectively out-lawing polygamy for all but the most extraordinary kind of man. Women scholars note that in modern times, some Muslim men choose to ignore or transgress against the last verse to suit their personal needs, to suit the convenience of their ego.

Non-Muslims may object that the Prophet himself had many more than the four wives permitted by the Qur'an, but the Holy Book has an answer for that. The verse, "O Prophet! We have made lawful to thee thy wives ..." (33:50), explains that he was extending the protection of marriage to women who were considered dis-cards in that society: slaves, widows, and divorcees. Of these, two were Jews and one was a Christian, once again illustrating the Prophet's spacious ability to dissolve cultural, social, and religious barriers. Before this period in his life, Muhammad broke the con-vention of his times by being in a monogamous relationship for twenty-five years with his beloved wife, Khadija. He undertook the other marriages only after she died.

The segregation of women in most mosques is contrary to the spirit of Islam. What is astonishing is that, in the early years of Islam, women had an unusually public role in the religious life of the community. In the seventh century, women helped build the first mosque in Medina. They performed the call to prayer, prayed alongside men, and sometimes led the ritual prayer. A woman, Umm Waarqa bint Abdullah, was especially trained by the Prophet himself to act as prayer leader for her whole tribe throughout her life.

Today, women are usually relegated to separate and inferior spaces in the mosque and not allowed to pray in the main sanctu-ary. What is telling is that all these traditions of secluding women arose from a medieval consensus among male jurists and clerics. It is incumbent on us as Muslims to reflect on the role of women in the first mosque of the Islamic world and take inspiration and guidance from that example. The Prophet proclaimed, "Women are the twin halves of men" and the Qur'an affirms: "For men and women who surrender themselves to God ... and for men and women who remember God unceasingly, for them God has readied forgiveness and a supreme recompense" (33:35).

Neither genital mutilation nor stoning for the crime of adultery are mentioned in the Qur'an. The former, reprehensible as it is, is based on tribal customs that predate Islam and exist entirely outside Islamic belief and practice. The latter became a "tradition" when Umar, the second caliph, instituted the practice. The caliph based his punishment on a number of weak ahadith and an extraordinary claim that a verse on stoning was revealed to the Prophet but was missing from the Qur'an.[8] Both the purported ahadith and the missing verse are inconsistent and contradictory because Qur'anic revelations allow adulterers and adulteresses to marry—something they most certainly could not do if they had been stoned to death.

There are many other ways in which institutional Islam ignores the Qur'an when it comes to women. It is ironic, say female Muslim scholars, that the Qur'an revolutionized the rights of women, but Islamic traditions discriminate against girls from the moment of "lamented" birth. A prime example is the Qur'anic condemnation of the heinous practice of female infanticide, which had been common in seventh-century Arabia. That practice may have been abolished, but today a terrible crime in Muslim countries is "honor killing" of women by male relatives. This murder is committed by a male relative who believes that the woman has brought shame on the family name by refusing to enter into an arranged marriage or by having a relationship that the family deems unacceptable. In another example, the Qur'an permits women to divorce, but Islamic legal rulings and customs in several Muslim societies have made it extremely difficult, both legally and socially, for women to leave their marriages.

For some reason, the tribal attitudes and customs of men in pre-Islamic Arabia still persist in the minds of many Muslim men worldwide. Perhaps it is because the men of Muhammad's time never got over their rage at having to cede human rights to women of the tribe. While the Prophet was alive, they stifled their objections, but once he died, male jurists reclaimed their dominance over women. As Islam spread rapidly to feudal societies all over the world, local patriarchal biases were reinforced. Some Muslim jurists and clerics today continue to invest in any number of false misogynistic ahadith concocted by religious scholars at the behest of unscrupulous rulers to justify their promiscuous lifestyle and mistreatment of women. And, shockingly, several Qur'anic verses that give women protection and advantage have been blatantly misinterpreted to favor men and oppress women.

One of the most shameful examples of this distortion is the way in which some Sharia courts supported by state legislation deal with rape cases brought by women. Amazingly, the rape victim can find herself charged not only with fornication or adultery but also with false accusation in some societies if she cannot produce four reliable people who witnessed the sexual penetration. Sharia is the guidance drawn primarily from the Qur'an and prophetic tradition. Interpretation of Sharia constitutes Islamic jurisprudence, and there are five schools of legal thought in Islam. Because interpretation varies even within the same school, there are a variety of different and, often, conflicting Sharia-derived rulings on women's rights. According to an exhaustive Gallup poll between 2001 and 2007 in thirty-five Muslim countries, a majority of women favor Sharia as one of the sources of legislation but complain bitterly that the Sharia rulings by men are starkly "non-Sharia compliant, " because they violate Islamic principles.[9]

The manmade interpretation of Sharia about rape is a gross misapplication of Qur'anic verses that were meant to protect women and safeguard their rights and honor:

And those who launch a charge against chaste women, and produce not four witnesses [to support their allegations]— flog them with eighty stripes; and reject their evidence ever after: for such men are wicked transgressors.

(24:4)

If any of your women are guilty of lewdness, take the evidence of four [reliable] witnesses from amongst you ...

(4:15)

In response to a particular incident involving Aisha, the Prophet's youngest wife, in which some men gossiped about adultery, the Prophet prayed for guidance and received a revelation: Henceforth, any accusation that a woman had committed adultery had to be corroborated by four reliable witnesses who saw the sexual act. Without the four witnesses, the woman could not be prosecuted. Furthermore, if the accuser could not produce the witnesses, he was guilty of slandering a chaste woman, and as punishment he would receive a number of lashes (24:4, 24:13). Far from chastening the men, this revelation seems to have distorted the thinking of some male jurists about women's rights. Thus, for example, in some Muslim societies, it is now the woman who must provide four witnesses when she is raped, and since this is virtually impossible, the rapist gets off scot-free or receives a light sentence under a lesser charge. Furthermore, if she becomes pregnant as a result of the rape, she is liable to be charged with fornication or adultery.

A glaring example of this travesty of justice is the rape law of Pakistan, instituted in 1979 to appease religious fundamentalists. The requirement of four witnesses to prove rape has caused untold pain, misery, and suffering to rape victims. Two well-known female activist lawyers, Asma Jahangir and Hina Jilani, describe the injustice as follows: "While the alleged rapist is innocent in the eyes of the law until proven guilty, the victim is presumed to be guilty until she proves her innocence."[10] Only after two-and-a-half decades of vigorous protests by women and human rights organizations did the Pakistani parliament finally amend the requirement of four witnesses in 2007 and allow rape cases to be tried by civil courts subject to the Pakistan penal code.

Many years ago, I saw my mother weep as she described her reverence for Prophet Muhammad's mission and vision, particularly the love and honor he accorded to women. "The rights of women are sacred," he used to say. "See that women are maintained in the rights granted to them." I can't help but think that the Prophet would weep if he saw how unjustly women are treated in some Muslim countries even today.

Core Teachings and Healing

For centuries the Muslim psyche has been half-paralyzed because of the restrictions placed on half the Muslim population. Thus it seems only fitting that Muslim women at last are healing and empowering themselves, and in the process may heal and empower all Islam. For the last few decades, Muslim countries have been the scene of exciting ferment and change, led by what is termed "women on the move." Women are challenging the stranglehold of the male medieval consensus and trusting in God to reclaim their rights. After the events of 9/11, the number of women wearing hijab (head covering, which is not mandatory in Islam) has increased exponentially—not because women have become more religious and submissive to their men, but because they have staked out an identity for themselves: Women are proclaiming that they are chaste, accountable to God, and eager to serve God's creation. They aspire to equal rights with men, not as defined in the West, but within the context of Islam.

Consistent with the Prophet's admonition to "seek knowledge from cradle to grave," unprecedented numbers of women are obtaining higher education, entering professional fields, and becoming scholars of the Qur'an. In most Muslim countries today, more women than men are enrolled in university. In Saudi Arabia, according to a 2010 United Nations report, 60 percent of university graduates are women and the percentage of female science graduates is higher than in the West. Forty percent of doctors are women, and 40 percent of private wealth is in the hands of women. In Iran, women PhDs outnumber men. In all Muslim countries, women are entering professions, including politics, previously dominated by men. Particularly exciting is a generation of female scholars steeped in knowledge of the Qur'an and Islamic jurisprudence and able to challenge the interpretations of male scholars.

Female theologians in the organization called Sisters in Islam have challenged the orthodox ulema (scholars and jurists) in Malaysia. In 2007 they succeeded in making marital rape a crime, and in 2009, a man was sentenced to five years in jail for forcing his wife to have sex with him. In India, a woman's organization called Bhartiya Muslim Mahila Andalon (Muslim Women's Association of India) recently decried religious decrees, called fatwas, issued by scholars and clerics of Darul Uloom Deoband, one of the largest and most prestigious religious education institutions in the Islamic world. The nonbinding rulings forbid women to talk loudly or ride bicycles, among other things, and deny women the right to become judges. The response of the women's organization is bold, direct, and powerful: "Who are you and what is your authority to pass such fatwas? In a secular democracy like India and in a religion that denounces clergyship, from where do you get the authority to pass dictates which are unconstitutional and un-Islamic?"[11]

Clearly, education is critical if all Muslims—men and women alike—are to live and work together as envisioned by the Prophet Muhammad. Too many Muslims are unaware of the Qur'anic verses guaranteeing women equal rights and an equal role in Islamic life. The Holy Book states: "And women shall have rights similar to the rights against them, according to what is equitable" (2:228), and proclaims, "We have conferred dignity on the children of Adam" (17:70). It is significant that on the Day of Judgment, the first question by God will be directed to the female infant buried alive, demanding to know why this terrible crime was committed. To many, female infanticide is also a metaphor for the forcible suppression of women's basic rights by men. The matter of oppression of women has the highest priority in the Divine Court. Equally significant is the fact that in the Qu'ran's version of the creation story, it is Satan who "beguiles" Adam and his spouse into making wrong choices, and there is no suggestion that the "woman" caused Adam to sin. Such is the boundless mercy of God that Divinity not only forgave both for their transgressions but appointed all men and women as God's vice-regents on earth (2:30).

Finally, we must discard the false misogynistic ahadith that have polluted minds and given birth to unacceptable traditions. In Pakistan, the second-most populous Muslim country in the world, Mohammad Ali Jinnah is revered as the "father of the nation." Most Pakistanis claim that he was uniquely instrumental, in the face of momentous obstacles, in the creation of Pakistan. In fact, it is against the law in Pakistan to criticize him. In a speech to the Muslim League meeting at Aligarh University in India, on March 10, 1944, he begged his fellow citizens to heed his words:

> No nation can rise to the height of glory unless your women are side by side with you. We are victims of evil customs. It is a crime against humanity that our women are shut up within the four walls of the houses as prisoners. There is no sanction anywhere for the deplorable conditions in which our women have to live.

It is not easy for men in patriarchal societies to become aware of their biases. Consider the famous story about the beloved ninth-century Iraqi sage Rabia, who was so exquisitely devoted to God that women and men adored her and clerics envied her. One day the clerics confronted Rabia and boasted: "The crown of prophet-hood has been placed on men's heads. The belt of nobility has been fastened around men's waists. No woman has ever been a prophet." "Ah," Rabia replied, "but egoism and self-worship and 'I am your

Lord most high' have never sprung from a woman's breast. All these have been the specialty of men."

Concluding Comments

We do not relinquish power easily, and this is as true of patriarchy as it is of political systems and all human institutions. As we awaken to our spiritual identity, it is simply obvious that equality is already real, even if not yet reflected in the world we share.

Sharing Our Stories

We enjoy the Q&A sessions that follow our presentations, because the questions reveal what people really want to know from us and how they hear our message. During these sessions, we stand side by side facing the audience—Ted on the left, Don in the middle, Jamal on his right. From our perspective, we stand in the order of the development of our traditions and believe that standing together is a physical demonstration of our message. (It also happens that Don is tall, and it looks better to have the two short guys like bookends on either side of him.)

One evening, we were feeling particularly happy that the audience was getting our message, and we were very pleased. It was a large audience, maybe 250 people. So far, all the questions had been very positive, reflecting a genuine concern for peace and the hope that the substance of religion could help move us along the path to peace.

Then a hand went up from the right side of the room near the back. A young woman stood and when the microphone was handed to her, she said in a tone that carried as much as her words did, "Why isn't one of you a woman?" The energy in the room shifted. Our euphoria evaporated.

We are always conscious that we are three men. Not just when we give our presentations. Always. Our ministries have, for each of us, been conducted during a time when the consciousness of the inequality of men and women has been dramatically raised, and we have done our best over the years to support the correction of that unequal status.

This was not the first time we had been asked this question, nor was it the first time we had thought about it and talked about it. And even though we know that all we can be is who we are, the question still makes us uneasy. Is it not okay to be who we are?

Pastor Don responded to the woman. "It is not that we are excluding a woman," he began. "It is that we are including each other." He gestured to his right and to his left. "When we started," he went on, "had our purpose been to achieve the kind of visibility that we have now, we might well have come together as two men and a woman. But we did not start our relationship with the intention of increasing our visibility. We started it because, despite the differences in our paths, we recognized something in each other that drew us together. We enjoyed each other's company. We became friends. It was in this context that we could explore what it would mean to develop the kind of trust that could break down the barriers that have separated us and come together in a way of cooperation and collaboration."

He paused for a moment before continuing. "Sometimes we think that the barriers are a reflection of masculine energy, and the collaboration a reflection of the feminine. We all have both within ourselves. We do our best to be aware of and to support the feminine energy of inclusivity in our work and our relationships."

The questioner sat down without further comment. It was not possible to tell how she felt about the answer. As far as we know, we've never found a way to respond to that question that seems to satisfy the one who asked it.

We are who we are. And we recognize and regret the conditions that make such a question still relevant. We see the need to move toward equality for men and women to be a major part of our work. Certainly, such equality is about justice as well as about making the most of our human resources. The perspectives of men and of women need to be combined in order to work cooperatively toward healing rather than suffering.

Questions for Discussion

- Have you always felt comfortable with your role as a man or woman in society? If so, why? If not, why not?

- Has your spiritual path spoken to you concerning the relative places of men and women? What teachings have you found? How do you feel about them?

- Do you think men and women need to have equal roles in society? How would it look were women to truly achieve equal status with men? What would the consequences be?

Spiritual Practices

From Jewish Tradition

Hebrew has no neuter form, so God is traditionally referred to as "He," even though God encompasses both the masculine and the feminine. Here the awkward pronouns are replaced with the nouns "God" and "humankind" for clarification.

> And God created humankind in God's image, in the Divine image God created humankind; male and female God created them.
>
> **(Genesis 1:27)**

> When God created humankind, God made humankind in the likeness of God; male and female God created them.
>
> **(Genesis 5:1–2)**

Meditate on these phrases that reflect the equality of men and women:

> I am created in the likeness of God.

> We are all created in the likeness of God.

From Christian Tradition

In the Lord's Prayer, which begins with the words *Our Father,* include the words *Our Mother* immediately following, and repeat the prayer to embrace both the masculine and the feminine. Using both pronouns allows us to take the equality of men and women more deeply into our spiritual awareness.

"Our Father, our Mother, who art in heaven, hallowed be Thy Name."

From Islamic Tradition

Since Arabic has no neuter form, everything is either masculine or feminine, and Allah is referred to in the masculine. But God is beyond gender, and encompasses both masculine and feminine energies. Whenever I read a verse containing the masculine pronoun relating to Allah, I also read that verse with a feminine pronoun. Repeat the following verse silently in meditation.

To Him belong the Most Beautiful Names.

(Qur'an 20:8)

To Her belong the Most Beautiful Names.

Chapter Four

Homophobia

A Denial of Legitimacy

The essential energy expressed in all spiritual traditions flows from oneness, love, and compassion. Consciousness awakens to oneness, the heart opens to love, and the body celebrates compassionate action in the world. Yet it is clear that oneness, love, and compassion are not doing so well in many religious institutions in our culture. The desire to be better, to be stronger, to have more control, eclipses oneness, impoverishes love, and leads us to act too often without compassion.

We have been conditioned in many ways by popular images of manhood and womanhood. Boys play with guns and girls play with dolls. When children choose the toys of the opposite sex, they are often met with resistance from their parents and their friends. Not only are we concerned with our basic sexual identity, but we are taught to compare ourselves to unrealistic media representations of men and women.

Religion has tended to support more traditional models of sexuality and of the marriage relationship. While reinforcing cultural norms, such a stance has often denied the needs of those who do not fit that traditional model. Problems arise when our religious affiliations and life experiences are in conflict with our personal truths. When our traditions fail to reflect our own integrity, the resulting tension can either drive us away from our religious affiliations or lead us to deny our inner realities in favor of the external demands of our faith. Unfortunately, when we deny our inner truth in order to remain within the institution, our denial of self festers within us like a wound. No matter how well-meaning the words and the rituals we observe, those teachings are no longer life-sustaining when we have to hide the truth of our being. This kind of secrecy can lead to acting out our anger in ways that are hurtful to ourselves and others.

The energy behind the religious condemnation of same-sex unions is, at this writing, still strong. Once again, we can question whether this condemnation is religion speaking or whether it is reflecting something else. Religions, even the most orthodox, do not prohibit men and women to marry even if they are unable or have chosen to have no children. All our traditions proclaim the central values of oneness, love, and compassion.

So when these core values are ignored in the condemnation of same-sex relationships, we need to question the source of that condemnation. We must encourage difficult conversations that can help us hear each other and ultimately support greater expressions of love. As troubling as those conversations may be, they are the best alternative to anger and unnecessary suffering.

Homophobia in Judaism
Personal Reflections

Homosexuality was not talked about much when I was growing up. I can't recall it ever being a subject of conversation at home or at school. In high school, there were boys who seemed to display feminine characteristics and who were called "fags," but I do not think I was aware of an actual homosexual person until I was in graduate school. What's odd about this is that when I was fifteen I had an older friend who was gay. I just didn't know it.

His name was Victor, and he taught at our temple. I can't remember how we got to be friends, but Victor took me and two other boys swimming at the Y and, what was more memorable, he secretly taught us to drive in his stick shift 1950 Studebaker. But whenever we went somewhere with Victor, I could sense uneasiness in my parents. I had no idea what the problem was, and they did not say.

Many years later, when I graduated from college and was about to enter rabbinical school, Victor sent me several expensive reference texts that I would need. His name was clearly stamped on the books. I realized later that he had begun rabbinical school only to be dismissed because his sexual orientation was not acceptable.

In my very first summer at the Hebrew Union College–Jewish Institute of Religion in Cincinnati, a friend and classmate suddenly disappeared after several weeks in the program. The faculty said nothing, and they would not respond to questions, except to say that he was okay. His classwork was good, so he had clearly not flunked out. Again, it only later occurred to me that he was rejected from the program for the same reason that Victor was not allowed to remain: Homosexuals could not be rabbis.

At the time of my rabbinic training, each first-year student had a required interview with a psychiatrist. I was uncomfortable with that session, but it never dawned on me that one of the prime objectives was to weed out those with unacceptable sexual orientations.

By the time I was ordained, I understood much more about homosexuality, at least as it was conceptualized in the late 1960s, but I did not yet have a close friend who was gay. Sometime in the early 1970s, that changed. One afternoon I received a call from a younger colleague on the East Coast. He was in the throes of a dilemma, and it related to his homosexuality. He wanted advice: Should he out himself with his congregation? Should he reveal his homosexuality to those in authority in the Reform movement?

I was deeply moved that he thought I was a safe person to talk to about this, and I remember urging him to follow the truth of his heart. He was the first gay friend with whom I could talk directly about homosexuality, and I learned a great deal from our conversations. Over the years, I have met other men and women who were conflicted about their alternative sexual orientations, as well as those who were able to celebrate it. I learned that homosexuality seemed to be hardwired into some people's very being. It was not a choice that could be "cured" by "right thinking" or by punishment.

In the 1980s, two events demonstrated this more deeply. One of my close classmates at seminary came to Los Angeles to join me in leading a spiritual retreat. At rabbinical school, he and I were two of the relatively few students who came to the graduate program already married. And he was the only one of us who already had a child. When we connected over the years, it was clear that he, like me, was pursuing a more spiritual path in his rabbinic work. What I had not counted on was the revelation that he had finally realized that he was gay. His coming out was filled with celebration for him, and it was very clear that he was relieved to reveal this truth of his being.

And in 1985, I was asked for the first time to officiate at a lesbian wedding. Friends of my sister in Massachusetts wanted to celebrate their relationship, and I agreed to meet with them and talk about officiating at such an event. Through our conversations, it became abundantly clear that their relationship was loving and deep, and that their commitment to each other was strong. If they had been a straight couple, there would be no doubt in my mind that I would be honored to officiate, and I realized that what was important was the love and the commitment they brought to their relationship—not their sexual orientation.

That ceremony preceded the more public debates on the subject of gay and lesbian unions in Reform rabbinical circles, but because there is no central authority in Reform Judaism, each rabbi is permitted to act from his or her personal learning and conscience. I performed that ceremony much as I performed marriages between men and women, and I did not make the distinction between a "commitment ceremony" and a "marriage."

I continue to learn about the significant relationships that can be formed and celebrated between people of the same sex as well as people of the opposite sex. In my counseling, as well as in my rabbinic work, I have now met with many homosexual and transgendered individuals and couples. If it weren't so reminiscent of people saying, "Some of my best friends are Jewish," I would say this of gays and lesbians. Suffice it to say that I do not experience the distinction between gay and straight to be one between "right" and "wrong." We are all seeking loving relationships in ways that are right for us. When we find a partner willing to engage in that endeavor, we are lucky indeed.

Scriptural and Institutional Support for Homophobia

The first biblical reference to homosexuality occurs in the nineteenth chapter of Genesis, when the men of Sodom demand that Lot send out his male visitors for the townsmen's sexual pleasure. Lot's visitors are angels in disguise and finally render the crowd blind to defuse that attack. Popular accounts of this biblical story focus on the destruction of Sodom and Gomorrah because of the moral corruption of the people there, leading to the belief that Judaism harshly punishes those who engage in homosexual acts. But, according to the text, the decision to destroy Sodom and Gomorrah had been made earlier, when the angels had visited Abram. Homosexuality was but one aspect of far greater problems with those two sinning cities.

The most common biblical texts used to condemn homosexual relationships are taken from the book of Leviticus. Although there is no mention of lesbian activity, sexual relations between men are forbidden:

Do not lie with a male as one lies with a woman; it is an abhorrence.

(Leviticus 18:22)

> If a man lies with a male as one lies with a woman, the two
> of them have done an abhorrent thing; they shall be put to
> death—their bloodguilt is upon them.
>
> *(Leviticus 20:13)*

During most centuries of Jewish life, homosexuality was simply
forbidden. There were too many commandments relating to family
life that could not be kept if one were in a homosexual relationship,
since that relationship could not produce children. This is still the
majority view in the more traditional Jewish communities.

In the liberal Jewish communities, gays and lesbians have not
only been accepted, but there are now openly gay rabbis and cantors
in Reform, Conservative, Reconstructionist, and Jewish Renewal
communities. I am grateful to have witnessed the transformation in
attitude and practice that has occurred over the forty-three years I
have been a rabbi. At the time of this writing, there is at least one
Orthodox rabbi who is openly gay, there have been gatherings of
Orthodox gays, but there is little indication now that the Orthodox
movement is willing to accept alternative sexual orientations.

Commentary on Homophobia

Much has been written about the two verses cited above from the
book of Leviticus. Interpretations of those verses basically support
the viewpoints of those who are doing the interpreting. So those
who believe that homosexuality is simply wrong can use the verses
literally to defend their position. Those who no longer believe
homosexuality to be unacceptable interpret the verses differently.
They suggest, for example, that a man *cannot* anatomically lie with
another man as he would lie with a woman. Because of this, both
verses can be seen to support what was the central value at that
time: the growth and strength of the tribal unit. It was crucial to
have more children because that was the only way the group could
survive. Homosexuality, or, for that matter, any sexual expression
that could not lead to conception, was forbidden. In a later age,

when the size of the tribe was not the primary concern for many Jews, less literal interpretations emerged.

I mentioned before that there are no biblical injunctions against lesbian activity. There are some who suspect a lesbian relationship in the story of Ruth and Naomi, and it's interesting that the commitment Ruth makes to Naomi is often used in heterosexual marriage ceremonies:

> For wherever you go, I will go; wherever you lodge, I will lodge; your people shall be my people, and your God my God. Where you die, I will die, and there I will be buried. Thus and more may the Lord do to me if anything but death parts me from you.
>
> *(Ruth 1:16b–17)*

Whether or not this reflects a sexual love relationship between the two women, it is not cited in Jewish literature as either impure or problematic. Perhaps because women's strong relationships with other women did not historically interfere with their childbearing potential, those relationships were not perceived as problems in either ancient or more modern texts. Today, however, lesbian relationships are as objectionable to traditionalists as gay unions.

Core Teachings and Healing

Judaism teaches that there is only one God who manifests as the entirety of Creation as well as awakens within each of us as the indwelling Presence. This is the proclamation of the *Sh'ma*, called the Watchword of our Faith, a prayer that is included at every worship service through the day and through the year:

> Listen, Israel, the Eternal One (Absolute Inclusive Being) is our God (the One Life awakening within each of us), the Eternal is One. Love the Eternal One your God with all your heart, with all your soul, and with all your energy.
>
> *(Deuteronomy 6:4–5; author's translation)*

In these lines of the *Sh'ma*, the realization of God's oneness leads to the expanded capacity to love. We are not talking in this chapter about casual sexual relationships between people but about relationships that bespeak love and commitment. When we trust our core values to point the way, we are able to honor love when it is shared between people.

At a certain point in the evolution of consciousness, we become aware that the love we experience is bigger than the particular relationship in which it manifests. When I love my partner and you love yours, we swim in the same waters of love. That love is the core value in intimate relationships.

Shalom bayit is one of the primary values in Jewish tradition. The phrase means "peaceful home" and is supported by many of the traditions of Jewish home life. You might remember that the root of the word *shalom* means "wholeness" and "completeness." It is this wholeness that undergirds the joy meant to be expressed in relationships of meaning and in our homes. This issue is far more crucial than the gender of our partner.

Homophobia in Christianity
Personal Reflections

My first experience with homophobia was the word *queer*. Of course, *queer* means strange. So I understood that somewhere on the fringes of my world existed people who were strange, possibly fearful. These were men who loved men. Women who loved women came into my consciousness later. What I didn't understand then was that the strangeness of queers was given to them by a culture that marginalized them, kept them in the shadows, in the closet. In my house, I don't remember any conversations about homosexuality. I do remember conversations about the importance of honoring the lives of all people.

It wasn't until I went to college that I began to be aware of homosexuality, albeit subtly. I knew that beneath the surface there was a culture of homosexuality, but I did not truly understand it. In seminary, it was more obvious. People were more willing to come out of the closet with people they could trust, and the reality of homosexuality began to emerge from the shadows. Then something dramatic happened.

During the ten years that I worked at the seminary, I encountered two pastors who confessed to me privately that they were gay and that, in fact, they were in closeted relationships. I remember trying to imagine what it must be like to live a life where one's love is not only a secret, it could—should it become known—end one's ministry. That reality is what moved the issue of homophobia from the shadows to the forefront of my own consciousness.

When I received an inquiry about moving to the University Congregational United Church of Christ of Seattle in 1994, I discovered that the congregation had recently called two gay men who were partners to become associate ministers. That call made the national news. I was in awe of the fact that the congregation had done something which, in those days, was unheard of. There weren't many openly gay pastors and certainly not any situations where a gay couple could both work at the same church.

When I accepted the position, and moved to Seattle, my two gay colleagues shared their stories with me. I felt two things simultaneously. First, I was genuinely "called" to this church in Seattle. Second, I felt inadequate to the practice of ministry in that new situation. In Hanover, New Hampshire, I had felt at least a small measure of confidence as I approached my ministry. It was another church on a college campus and since I had lived on or near a college campus for my entire life, I felt I understood something of the culture and could move forward there with ministry. But in Seattle, I was entering a new space altogether. Initially, I told the church council that I would not be using the title "senior minister" and that my colleagues (two gay men and a woman) would no longer be "associate ministers." This form of hierarchy undermined my colleagues. Eventually, we called this form of ministry "team ministry," but at the time, it was simply a way of giving two gay men and a straight woman (people who had been previously denied visibility) opportunities to publicly practice ministry.

The gay and lesbian community in our congregation was very generous and patient with me, and I learned several crucial lessons—lessons that became essential tools for my ministry. First, they were not joining the congregation because they were hoping that it would become a "gay" church. They became members of the congregation because they wanted to worship in a place where they could be accepted as whole human beings. Second, they had not chosen to be gay or lesbian, transgendered or bisexual. They were who they were because they were born that way, and what they wanted was the opportunity to have fruitful, loving, and open relationships—a basic human right.

Over time I began to take for granted that there would be people in the congregation who were homosexuals and that there would be gay and lesbian men and women on the pastoral and administrative staffs. Eventually, I became the only straight person on the leadership team. The blessing of this experience extends well beyond the particularity of homosexuality. It taught me the pain of exclusion because of a fact of birth (just as, for example, the color of one's skin is a fact of birth) and strengthened my resolve to proclaim the Gospel of Jesus as a Gospel of inclusion.

Scriptural and Institutional Support for Homophobia

Even for Christian people, the famous passage in the Holiness Code found in the book of Leviticus is a major source for this topic: "You shall not lie with a male as with a woman; it is abomination" (18:22). The Holiness Code functioned as a guide to living for the Hebrew people as they began their new lives in the land of Canaan. Note that the verse is directed solely to men and solely to Hebrew men in Canaan. Many Christian people today, objecting to gay marriage and to homosexuality in general, cite this verse as an absolute transcription of the voice of God.

In the Christian Scriptures, Paul's letter to the church at Rome says, "For the wrath of God is revealed from heaven against all ungodliness and wickedness of those who by their wickedness suppress the truth" (Romans 1:18). The suggestion that this idea of wickedness refers to homosexuality is verified in some later verses in that same chapter: "Their women exchanged natural intercourse for unnatural and also their men, giving up natural intercourse with women, were consumed with passion for one another. Men committed shameless acts with men" (Romans 1:26–27a).

And in Paul's letter to the church in Corinth he brings up similar themes: "Do you know that wrongdoers will not inherit the Kingdom of God? Do not be deceived! Fornicators, idolaters, adulterers, male prostitutes, sodomites, thieves, the greedy, drunkards, revilers, robbers—none of these will inherit the Kingdom of God" (1 Corinthians 6:9–10).

There are various other references in the letters of Paul that have been used to support an active opposition to homosexuality, but the references above from both the Jewish and Christian Scriptures function as primary references.

Through the ages, the Christian church has consistently defined homosexuality as a sin and has called on adherents to avoid homosexual behavior and to avoid contact with homosexual people. It has also barred membership in a church or leadership in a church to homosexual people. Sometimes this opposition has been limited to exclusion, but sometimes, as in Nazi Germany, it has expanded to violence and death. The fear and condemnation of homosexuality is a strong part of the history of Christianity. It has only been since the latter half of the twentieth century that some churches have begun to rethink the relationship between homosexuality and sin.

Commentary on Homophobia

In Christianity, homophobia arose at a time when it appeared to threaten the essential structure of society by undermining the place and authority of the family and the perpetuation of humanity. The unfortunate juxtaposition of homosexuality and other events associated with the breakup of a culture, such as orgies and drunkenness, furthered that sensibility. In addition, the fear of homosexuality included the conviction that people were able to choose whether or not to be gay or lesbian, transgendered or bisexual.

Today, we know that two people of the same gender are as capable of a committed relationship with each other as a man and a woman are—as long as the surrounding culture supports the relationship. We also know that children can be raised very effectively by two people of the same gender. When there is cultural support, homosexuality poses no threat to the stability of a culture. In fact, because it is no longer a secret, homosexuality in committed relationships contributes to the strength and health of a culture.

We also know from science that most people have no choice in their sexual orientation (thus the word *preference* is a misnomer). People are what they are. Because homosexuality is not a threat to a culture, does no harm to anyone, and is a blessing to those whose orientation defines them as homosexuals, it should be seen as an important component for a healthy, productive, and imaginative culture.

Core Teachings and Healing

As we keep saying, while each of our traditions has a particular emphasis (Judaism: oneness; Christianity: unconditional love; Islam: compassion), all three of these core teachings exist in each of our traditions. And it is not a coincidence that oneness precedes unconditional love and that they both precede compassion. We have to have a sense of oneness and unconditional love in order to have the will to be compassionate beings.

But we must also be able to empathize with the lives of other people, especially people who are different from us. Imagination is a tool that can help us to empathize, when used in the context of these three core teachings. People who are not gay or lesbian, transgendered or bisexual, have a difficult time understanding what it must be like to have such sexual orientations and, at the same time, to feel so entirely excluded from the dominant culture. An understanding of the core teachings can help us see that the opposition to homosexuality by the Christian church points to the need to overcome the fear that the masculinity of the culture would be weakened by the acceptance of homosexuality. In fact, the culture stands to be strengthened and healed by embracing those with a homosexual orientation. For example, if men did not fear what straight men perceive to be an inherent "weakness" (when compared to the macho sensibility the culture associates with straight men), one of the bases for fear of homosexuality would disappear. That fear keeps men from becoming themselves fully because it blocks our ability to celebrate the differences, the various sexual orientations into which we are born.

Living in that fear keeps us in a kind of "distant country," suggested in the parable of the prodigal son, where we don't become fully ourselves until we come "home." We come home and receive the forgiveness born of unconditional love. And what we need forgiveness for, in this case, is not for being gay. The forgiveness we need as a culture and a world is for thinking that homosexuality is anything but natural. And this forgiveness is not needed because we are bad people, but because we need to start over in our thinking about homosexuality.

In effect, we need to be born again to a different and positive and supportive sensibility concerning homosexuality. The fear and condemnation of homosexuality points to a greater fear in us that does indeed need healing. It points to our uncertainty about the value and strength of our essential humanity along with the essential dignity that is a feature of every human being. Loving without conditions is a way of living effectively with that uncertainty.

Homophobia in Islam

Personal Reflections

As a child I delighted in tales of the prophets who preceded the Prophet Muhammad. One fourth of the Qur'an is replete with such stories, and my teachers in religious school mined them for spiritual and moral insights. One story, however, was not so delightful to my classmates and me. This was the episode of Lut (called Lot in the Hebrew Bible) and the people of Sodom and Gomorrah (7:80–84). The Qur'anic version differs from the biblical story in that Lut was not only the single decent man living in "sin city"; he was actually a prophet, sent to warn the people about their lewdness, involving "transgressing beyond bounds" (7:81).

This story was just too bizarre for us naïve young kids to comprehend. How was it possible that every male member of a community would "sodomize" male visitors who came to their town? Didn't they have parents or elders who would restrain them? What was sodomy, anyway? And no matter how abominable the crime committed by the men, why should women and children also die in a shower of brimstone?

After class, we consulted our older friends, who filled us in about the ghastly crime of sodomy. That led to more questions in class the next day. How could a man be sexually interested in other men, we kept asking the teacher, since that seems so unnatural? The teacher answered that such men lack self-restraint and allow their evil desires to fester until they choose the sin rather than submit their wills to God. Such deviants, he assured us, are few in number and live mostly in Western countries. The main lesson of the story of Lut, he concluded, is that if you have homosexual thoughts and act on them, the All-Merciful God will destroy you.

But then we had another burning question. Knowing that the men were so deviant, why would the prophet Lut offer them his daughters in marriage? What kind of a father was he? Again our teacher fumbled for an answer. The verse was metaphorical, he said. The prophet would never literally give his daughters away in marriage to these transgressors. The verse was only meant to teach that we should choose women as sexual partners because they are "purer for you" (11:78). Relieved, we were ready to be done with this story and move on to another prophet. We had absorbed the lesson: Homosexuality is an abominable sin, and God will get you if you commit it.

For nearly a decade, I never gave the subject another thought, until a classmate disclosed that he was gay, and I discovered how deeply I had absorbed the lesson of Lut. Reflexively, I judged him to be morally weak and polluted, and I resolved to have little to do with him. Though always polite, I limited our contacts and never spent time alone with him. This was to be my policy with all gays and lesbians I encountered: Be polite but keep a safe distance.

All that changed dramatically following a conversation with my sister, a medical doctor in Bangladesh. She told me about a thirty-year-old man who trembled with trepidation as he told her about his "ailment." Since childhood he had been attracted to male partners, and he was filled with shame and anguish. For a decade he had tried prayer, fasting, and repentance. Holy men called *fakirs* and *pirs* had performed all kinds of rituals and exorcisms on him but to no avail. With tears in his eyes he begged my sister for any medicine or surgery that could cure him of his illness. My sister, a woman of great wisdom and compassion, reassured him that he was not ill or insane and was able to put him in touch with agencies that provide counseling and practical solutions on issues of homosexuality in a Muslim society.

This story moved my heart to suspend judgments about gays, especially about Muslim homosexuals, who suffer under the suffocating burden of their secret. Muslims who reveal or act on their homosexual impulses are subject to hostility and sometimes violence from their community, clerics, and even members of their own families. By now a co-minister of the Interfaith Community Church in Seattle, I welcomed homosexuals into my congregation and was eager to learn about their lives.

But I confess that I had, at the time, ulterior motives. I was determined to identify factors leading to their same-sex interest and, out of compassion, to help them with reparative therapy. I believed I could "reverse the wiring" if I applied the Sufi psychology skills that I had learned from my father. I had been building up a good reputation in my "sacred psychology" practice and had enjoyed a fair measure of success with clients who had problems with depression, sexual abuse, and various addictions. I was eager to work with a gay client and help that person become the straight person God intended him or her to be.

One fateful afternoon, a Muslim family came to me in great distress about their twenty-year-old son who had an "addiction problem." They had heard about my successes and were confident I could help. It turned out that the addiction issue was, in fact, homosexuality. He didn't want to be gay, he said, and he was eager to undo the pain he was causing his family. The mother had threatened to commit suicide, and they were all in deep distress, but I was energized. I was going to help a Muslim homosexual and God was going to help me with my therapy to heal and "fix" this well-meaning son.

Over a long period of treatment I showered the young man with boundless compassion as I prayerfully utilized every modality I knew. Every week I gave him a variety of psychological and spiritual practices as "homework" while I myself read all I could about homosexuality. As the weeks and months passed, the young man reported feeling more peaceful and closer to God, but he experienced no change in his sexual preference.

Despite my abiding faith that my client could be "rewired," I had to inform his parents that it wasn't happening on my watch. Deeply disappointed, they decided to consult with well-known Muslim spiritual leaders and psychologists both in the United States and in select Muslim countries.

A few months later, they were back in my consulting room, angry. Their son had talked to many Islamic teachers, whose advice consisted of lectures about doing the "inner jihad," that is, fighting the inner demons. According to these teachers, one must discard the "hypothalmus issue" and the theory of "genetic propensity." The noble spirit of Islam and the undisputed gene of self-control will dissolve unnatural feelings and tendencies, they said, all this by the grace of God. The son had listened dutifully and undergone several "reparative" therapies and tailor-made spiritual rituals, but to no avail. Finally, suffering from excessive guilt and depression, he had tried to kill himself. This desperate action awakened his parents, who realized that they just wanted him to stay alive and be happy. They decided to accept his unconventional lifestyle and try to understand him. Today, their son has a loving male partner and his relationship with his parents is, to quote his words, "more authentic and affectionate than ever."

Scriptural and Institutional Support for Homophobia

Consistent with my boyhood experience in religious school, the Islamic view on homosexuality is rooted in the Qur'anic story about Sodom and Gomorrah in a handful of verses (7:80–84, 11:77–83, 15:57–77, 26:160–174, 27:54–58, 29:28–35). The issue can be summarized in the following verses: "Of all the creatures in the world, will ye approach males, and leave those whom God has created for you to be your mates? Nay, ye are a people transgressing (all limits)" (26:165). And, "Would ye really approach men in your lusts rather than women? Nay, ye are a people (grossly) ignorant!" (27:55). For their evil actions, all the people of Sodom and Gomorrah were destroyed by fire and brimstone, and "verily in this is a sign" (26:174). The sign, according to some Islamic scholars, is that God will not tolerate the "abominable" practice of homosexuality. Interestingly, lesbian acts are not mentioned in the Qur'an.

As Islam spread and laws were being codified during the time of the caliphs in the seventh century, questions arose about the punishment for committing gay and lesbian acts. It was clear from the ahadith that such acts were forbidden: "When a man mounts another man, the throne of God shakes," and, "Lesbianism by women is adultery between them."[1] But what should be the punishment? Again a hadith seems to supply an answer: "Kill the one who sodomizes and the one who lets it be done to him."[2] But no companion of the Prophet could recall any punishment that he actually pronounced on gays and lesbians.

It was the first caliph, Abu Bakr, who condemned a homosexual to death by crushing him beneath a wall of debris. This is the only precedent from early times, and conservative jurists use it to equate the crime of homosexuality with adultery, for which the punishment is death. It is worth noting that the burden of proof for a homosexual crime is the same as that for adultery: Charges must be supported by four reliable witnesses who saw the physical act. Homosexuality is punishable by death in Saudi Arabia, Iran, Mauritania, Sudan, Nigeria, and Yemen. A contemporary, conservative Islamic jurist, Yusuf al-Qaradawi, acknowledges that the penalty may seem severe and extreme, but he justifies it by saying that it will "maintain the purity of the Islamic society and keep it clean of perverted elements."[3] In practice, imposition of the death penalty is quite uncommon except in Iran and, under the Taliban, in Afghanistan. Even in Saudi Arabia, the authorities prefer to impose fines or jail time unless someone is openly launching a movement to promote the cause of gays and lesbians.

In most of the Muslim world, institutional Islam is hostile to homosexuality but considers it to be a moral disorder that can be reversed. Just as no one is born a liar or thief, the institutional opinion is that no one is born a homosexual. This disorder occurs as a result of improper parental guidance, poor religious education, and a promiscuous environment. Just as addiction to gambling and alcohol can be overcome, so can the addictive urges of homosexuality. Gays and lesbians who seek help are encouraged to keep their "addictive feelings" to themselves and even enter into heterosexual marriages. Conventional wisdom is that leading a "normal and ethical life" will bring about a cure by purifying, healing, and aligning those feelings to moral goodness. The pressure to conform is enormously and painfully high.

Commentary on Homophobia

Several years ago, while conducting a workshop retreat about the status of women and homosexuals in our respective Holy Books, my Interfaith Amigos and I suddenly burst out laughing. At the same instant, each of us had recognized the absurdity of the situation: None of us was either female or homosexual, yet here we were, speaking as experts on the subject. No matter how open-minded and inclusive we might think we are, we will always have an inherently male and heterosexual bias. We can never truly do justice in interpretation of scripture on behalf of women and homosexuals. Once again, the time-honored adage rings true: "We do not see things as they are; we see things as we are." With this caveat in mind, let us try to explore the issue of homosexuality from a gay Muslim point of view.

Muslim gays, like their Jewish and Christian counterparts, point out that the story of Sodom and Gomorrah is not about homosexuality but about male assault, rape, and violence against a traveling guest, and as people of principle they naturally condemn such acts. Legitimate homosexual relationships, they insist, are based on consensual love and tenderness. They believe that the oft-quoted verses on spousal love in the Qur'an, such as "He created for you mates from among yourselves, that ye may dwell in tranquility with them and He has put love and mercy between your hearts" (30:20–21), apply equally to straight and gay couples. Like most heterosexuals, they also believe in the sacredness and tenderness of union and would like to dwell in tranquility but with a same-sex partner. They believe that God created them as they are; they did not choose their orientation, God chose for them.

The penalty for homosexual acts is not specified in the Qur'an. The Hanafi School of Law (the largest in the Muslim world) has concluded that there is no physical punishment for the sin of homosexuality and the prescription of death has no Qur'anic basis. Similarly, the death penalty mentioned in the hadith goes against the spirit of the Holy Book. This is, in any case, a weak, unsubstantiated hadith that conservative jurists may have fabricated for convenience. The medieval punishments meted out to homosexuals—horrific deaths by being crushed, burned, or thrown from a minaret—are not in alignment with the Qur'an and must be condemned. The primary source of guidance for Muslims is the Qur'an, and any extra-Qur'anic source must conform to the spirit of the Holy Book. Rightly guided caliphs are only human beings and are capable of mistakes. It is an Islamic duty to speak out against punishment that is not rooted in the Holy Qur'an.

Core Teachings and Healing

One day I was speaking with an imam about the very small community of Muslim gays and lesbians in town and asked if it might be possible to integrate them into his congregation. "Never!" he exclaimed, banging his fist on the table. "Never! Never will a homosexual be accepted in Islam. They are perverts. They are not Muslims." The severity of his reaction surprised me. But rather than debate our conflicting views on the subject of homosexuality, I tried to explain that our goal should be to follow the dictates of the Qur'an when dealing with someone whose views and practices are opposed to our own. Only God can judge who is a true Muslim, says the Qur'an, and the respected scholar Tariq Ramadan says that, "When a person pronounces the attestation of the Islamic faith and becomes a Muslim, if that person engages in homosexual practices ... no one has a right to drive him or her out of Islam."[4]

It is essential to emphasize here that in dealing with someone whose beliefs are diametrically opposed to our own, the Qur'an tells us to be gracious and generous: "Invite [all] to the Way of thy Lord with wisdom and beautiful preaching; and argue with them in ways that are best and most gracious" (16:125). The Holy Book also warns us not to slander anyone, no matter how disagreeable that person might be to us, and Islamic sages offer advice similar to that found in Jewish and Christian writings: "Veil the faults of others, so yours might be veiled." The true measure of a person's worth, the Qur'an says, is humility and a heart turned in sincere devotion to the unseen God (50:33).

By all conservative estimates, 6 percent of the world's population is homosexual, from which we may infer that a similar percentage of Muslims are gay. When this particular imam insisted that God would be pleased with them only if they did the work of "inner jihad," I suggested that we straight Muslims needed to do the same work, emphasizing that, in the theory of *tawhid* (oneness), homosexuals are part of God's community, and it is our duty to integrate that 6 percent of Muslims into the *Ummah* (Islamic community). We could do this "little by little."

This concept of gradual understanding and acceptance is a divine theme that runs consistently through the Qur'an. God even invokes the elements of nature to illustrate the point: "So I call to witness the rosy glow of sunset, the night in its progression, and the moon as it grows into fullness: Surely you shall travel from stage to stage. What, then, is the matter with them, that they do not have faith in the unfolding?" (84:16–19). The revelation of the Qur'an itself was a little-by-little process requiring twenty-three years so that the gradual revelations might "strengthen the heart" (25:32).

There are several instances of this progression. Slavery was such a deeply rooted practice in the seventh century that the Qur'an did not prohibit it with a single revelation. Instead, it declared that the highest act of charity was the freeing of a slave from bondage. By the time of the Prophet's death, the institution of slavery had been weakened, but not abolished. God gives us time to grow in consciousness and for societal conditions to change progressively.

Is it not possible that what was prohibited then is now permissible? Take, for example, the prohibition against mutilation of the human body. Declaring that the body is sacred in Islam, the Prophet strictly forbade the savage custom of mutilating the bodies of slain enemies during battle. Hundreds of years later, when autopsy became an accepted medical tool, many Muslim scholars and jurists forbade it vehemently, citing the Prophet's words about the sanctity of the human body. But today, knowing that autopsy can advance the cause of medical science and help save lives, the jurists now permit it.

We may assume that the Qur'an would call on us to expand our understanding and find ways to integrate our homosexual brothers and sisters into our hearts and into the community. "Make room for one another in your collective life," the Qur'an urges; "do make room: [and in return] God will make room for you [in His Grace]" (58:11). Expansion of our consciousness is a sacred duty, and there should be no limit to our capacity for compassion, awareness, and inclusivity. We can never repeat too many times the Qur'anic verse that God has created diversity so that we might "come to know the other" (49:13). Sadly, I have found that the imams and other members of the Islamic community who are so outspoken against homosexuals have not taken this verse to heart; not one of them has bothered to get to know a single homosexual personally.

It is telling that conservative Jews and Christians also interpret passages from their Holy Books to declare same-sex acts abominable, and they get just as inflamed as conservative Muslims do when asked to soften their views on homosexuality. Even so, poll numbers show that over the past few decades a significant number of fundamentalists in America have accepted homosexuals. What has made them less homophobic?

In a groundbreaking book titled *American Grace*,[5] social scientists Robert Putnam and David Campbell argue that the "bridge model" has wrought this change. Over the decades, people who are, by and large, conservative Christians have made friends with their colleagues at work and in their social lives without realizing that they were gay. As the political and social conditions changed in this country, and homosexuals felt safer in disclosing their same-sex orientation, the rigid moral judgments of their heterosexual friends and colleagues lost their harshness because personal relationships of mutual respect had already been established. People all over America found that they knew and liked gay and lesbian people—they just hadn't known them as such. As in the Qur'anic examples cited earlier, verses in the scriptures haven't changed, but attitudes have shifted. Commenting on the authors' findings, Robert Wright, in a *New York Times* op-ed, writes, "The meaning of scripture is shaped by social relations."[6]

It is time for Muslims and Islamic institutions, out of love, compassion, and awareness, to begin to "come to know the other." This prescription is a Qur'anic injunction.

Concluding Comments

The core teachings of each of our traditions urge us to appreciate more deeply the integrity of our being. When this integrity encompasses nonheterosexual behavior, our religions are challenged to move beyond exclusivist pronouncements to honestly understand those whose sexuality does not conform to the norm.

Our religious traditions do not favor homosexuality, largely because the primary concern has been on increasing the strength and numbers of our communities. Until recent times, same-sex relationships did not include raising children. But it is clear that we are encouraged to open our hearts to those with alternative sexual orientations, so that we might better understand and appreciate them. It is time for us to more openly celebrate all relationships that contribute to the expansion of love in our world.

Sharing Our Stories

While people during the Q&A sessions that follow our presentations are often rather outspoken, on occasion there are questions that are too personal for them to raise in front of a group.

One evening, after the formal program was over, we noticed a middle-aged couple hanging back a bit from the people gathered around us. When we talked about it later, we learned that each of us had wondered if there was something the couple wanted or needed. They seemed hesitant, unsure about what to do. After a while, the crowd around us thinned, and we saw the woman whispering to the man. Then she gave him a small push in our direction.

"Hi," said the man, putting out his hand. "I'm Doug. This is my wife Ellen (not their real names, of course). We really enjoyed your program." We shook hands with them. There was an awkward silence as we waited to learn what it was that had caused both his reluctance and her need to have him talk to us. We tried to look encouraging.

Ellen shot her husband a glance.

"There's something I'd like to ask you about," he said at last. "I hear you talk about homosexuality," he almost stumbled over the word, "and how it's looked at differently today than it used to be." He glanced at Ellen. She nodded.

"For my whole life, I thought they—homosexuals, gay people—were really dangerous. Diabolical even. That's what everybody I knew said. And I taught my kids the same way. I think I said some pretty horrible things about homosexuals."

Suddenly, he looked more sad than uncomfortable. He took a breath.

"I was pretty harsh," he said. "But I've been thinking about it a lot lately, and starting to wonder. Maybe I was wrong. And now I come here tonight and hear what you three are saying. It's as if you're giving me permission to admit that they're are not as bad as I had thought."

Ellen edged a little closer to him and took his hand. Doug took another deep breath. "You see," he said, "we think our son is gay. He's never said anything about it to us, but we think that's because he's afraid because of all the terrible things I've said over the years."

Doug looked down at the floor, as if it had taken all his energy to get those words out, and now he was listening to them reverberating in the sudden silence.

After a moment, Ellen said, "Doug's a really good man. He's been a great father. Bill looks up to him, and I know he doesn't want to disappoint his dad. So we think that's why he's hiding who he is and pretending to be someone he isn't. It's really painful to watch and we don't know how to talk to him about it."

Their honesty and their anguish were palpable. They looked at us hopefully and expectantly. It was one of those moments that clergy have all too often in which we wish we had easy answers, verbal Band-Aids to put on internal wounds. We looked at each other. Now it was our turn to take a deep breath or two.

Ted was the first to speak. "I'm impressed by your honesty, Doug, and I'm deeply honored that you are sharing this with us. Clearly, real communication needs to begin, and you have started the process by talking to us. What's important is to create space in which dialogue can happen."

"Maybe," Don said, "you can use tonight's program as a way to do that. Perhaps you could tell the truth, and talk about hearing a rabbi, a pastor, and an imam teaching that homophobia is inconsistent with the true core teachings of all three of their faiths. You might say that you had been reconsidering your previous views even before you came to the program tonight, but what you heard here kind of opened your eyes and opened your heart. And you want him to know that you are sorry for the harsh way you judged homosexuality in the past."

"I'd advise you to share that without expecting any response from him," Jamal said in his usual gentle voice. "You just want him to know that you feel very differently than you used to. You could say that even an old dog can learn something new." We all smiled.

A month or so later, we got an e-mail from Doug:

Dear Interfaith Amigos,

I'm writing to tell you what happened after our conversation. It took a couple of weeks, but I finally got up the nerve to talk to Bill. He didn't say anything then or for the next few days, and I wondered if I'd said something wrong and made things worse. It was a tough few days.

Finally, last night, Bill sat us down after dinner. He asked if I was serious about what I'd said to him about how I'd changed my thinking. I said that I certainly was. And then he began to talk to us about his sexual identity and how hard it's been for him. It seems he's known he was different for a very long time, and he thought he was a little crazy. He thought he'd outgrow it. He tried to deny that he found him-self attracted to other boys rather than to girls. He cried. We all cried. And then, when I hugged him after our talk, he really hugged me back for the first time in a very long time.

I want you to know how much your words meant to me and my family. Thank you so much.

Doug

P.S. Bill wanted me to say, Thank you, for him, too.

When something like this happens, the rightness of our work is deeply affirmed. We are all grateful to Doug for sending that e-mail.

Questions for Discussion

- Was there anything in this chapter that surprised you? What was it? Did it encourage you to think differently about your own attitudes?

- Was there any particular event or person in your life that changed your views regarding homosexuality? What happened? How did you change?

- Homosexuality is a hot-button issue, with arguments for and against same-sex marriage. If you were to argue in favor of the side of this issue you currently oppose, what would you say?

Spiritual Practices

From Jewish Tradition

There is a special blessing to be recited when in the presence of someone who is different from us. "Blessed are You, Eternal Being, our indwelling God, Universal Creative Presence, Who makes creatures different." Through blessing we celebrate peaceful diversity. Here is a phrase to use in meditation: "We are differently blessed." You might recite this silently when you're with other people, affirming our uniqueness without judgment.

From Christian Tradition

Meditate on this verse from the Gospel of John: "And this is my commandment, that you love one another as I have loved you." Remember that unconditional love embraces everyone—it is not conditional on their actions or their beliefs. This is a perfect opportunity to open our hearts to those who are different from us.

From Islamic Tradition

The Qur'an admonishes us again and again, "Listen!" and "Pay attention!" We have the opportunity to listen to those who are different from ourselves, and we also have the opportunity to pay attention to the deepest truths of our own being. Meditate upon these continually repeated refrains from the Qur'an and become more available to listen to the life stories, and sometimes even the anguish, of those who are different from you.

Chapter Five

Underneath It All

God and Revelation

Our understanding of God and revelation provides the foundation for our willingness to share the difficult topics in the traditions that inform our lives. Our traditions comprise the three Abrahamic faiths, each an expression of ethical monotheism, the belief in oneness that awakens us to ethical action in the world. Each of our traditions has a basic sacred text. In one way or another, these texts are understood as expressions of the One. We will focus on our beliefs concerning the nature of Divine Being in this chapter, and we will talk a little about difficulties with the word *God*.

The relationship between Divine Being and our sacred texts is expressed through revelation. This is the second of the major concerns that we hope to address here. *Revelation* refers to the communication between Divine Being and human beings. One of the major difficulties we confront has to do with the relative divine origins of our sacred texts. There have been times in history when violence erupted because of conflicting claims of authenticity. So it is crucial that we consider these issues in the context of our expanding interfaith dialogue.

Rabbi Ted's Reflections on God and Revelation

There is perhaps no word that historically has given us as much trouble as the three-letter word *God*. Too often used to threaten or to promise, the word frequently conjures up the image of some giant perfect person, usually male, who is in control of everything. When pictured as a kindly wise man in celestial garb, such a representation can bring solace and comfort. When seen as an angry and avenging heavenly person who punishes and controls, this personification inspires insecurity and fear. But perhaps such images are more reflections of our own being than accurate representations of an inclusive Divine Being in whom all else exists.

The word *God* refers to ultimate reality and the ultimate mystery of our existence. Here's my elevator speech concerning this Divine Being: God is everything that exists and infinitely more. God is the container that holds us all, and God is the spirit of life awakening within each of us.

If the elevator is a slow one, I might add one of my favorite verses from the Hebrew Bible: "It has been clearly demonstrated to you, so that you know that the Eternal One alone is God; nothing else exists" (Deuteronomy 3:35, translation according to insights of the more mystical Hasidic traditions). Our universe—or as our knowledge expands—our multi-verse, is part of a living Being that is all that is. Everything that exists is made of "God-stuff." As my friend and teacher, Rabbi David Cooper, says, the universe is always "God-ing."[1]

We are all expressions of this one Life, so we are always interconnected with one another and with all that is. On a physical level, we contain elements that are part of the natural world; on a mental level, we can attain wisdom that is greater than our individual mind; on the spiritual level, we open to an awareness beyond our individuality to realize ever-expanding dimensions of the One.

It is difficult to name such an all-inclusive reality, because all names limit that which is named. It's as if we draw a circle around anything we name and say, "Everything within this circle belongs to this name. Everything outside the circle is something else." But what are we to do when we are referring to something that is both *inside* and *outside* such a circle?

It was in response to this awareness of the limitation of words, that, sometime in the third century BCE, the decision was made to no longer pronounce the most holy Hebrew four-letter name of God. There are many names for God in Hebrew but this four-letter name, which became known as the tetragrammaton (which means "four-letter name") is unique in its universality.

That name-which-is-not-pronounced consists of the four Hebrew letters *yod-hay-vav-hay* and is a form of the three-letter verb root *hay-yod-hay*, which means "to be." The unspoken name, comprising these four letters, can best be translated "That which Is." The name refers to Being without limitation of time or space.

Since the tetragrammaton occurs so often in the Hebrew Bible and in Jewish worship, it was decided that a substitute word, *Adonai*, be read whenever it was encountered. The Hebrew vowels for the replacement word, which contains five letters, were placed within the four letters that were not to be read. Any reader of Hebrew would see that the word could not be read as written, since no letter can be read with more than one vowel, and would be reminded to replace it with *Adonai*, which is translated as *Lord*. This replacement word is far less inclusive than the four-letter name, and can be used when referring to a person as a sign of respect. A form of the same word, *adoni*, has been used the way we use *sir* in English. In the most current Jewish Publication Society translation of the Hebrew Bible used in this book, *Adonai* is translated in small caps: Lord, to remind us that *Adonai* is just a placeholder word. *Adonai*, or Lord, is far too small a name when referring to the Being that includes us all.

There is another form of this name of God that can be spoken. It is the name that Moses heard in response to his unique question:

Moses said to God, "When I come to the Israelites and say to them, 'The God of your fathers has sent me to you,' and they ask me, 'What is His name?' what shall I say to them? And God said to Moses, "Ehyeh-Asher-Ehyeh."

(Exodus 3:13–14a)

Remember that, because Hebrew has no neuter, everything spoken is either masculine or feminine. God, like everything else, can be a "He" or a "She," but not an "It." Perhaps this can remind us that the universe is alive, and that masculine and feminine energies are part of the whole and also part of each of us.

Ehyeh is the first-person-singular pronoun of the Hebrew verb *to be,* and in biblical Hebrew can include past, present, and future. *Ehyeh* is the *I* without limitation of time or space—the absolutely inclusive and universal *I. Asher* is a connective word that means "as" or "that." So the most exact translation of the name Moses heard is "I AM as I AM." God is the universe opening its *I.* The first-person pronoun alone is unitive; every other pronoun reflects a duality. A *he* demands a *she*, a *you* demands a *me*, a *we* demands a *they.* So God, as the universal singular *I*, is the unitive identity of the universe.

Our own *I*, closer to us than breathing, is the individualized expression of the universal inclusive *I.* Because God awakens through each of us, God is the only Being who can celebrate all religious paths at once, speak all languages at the same time, and be present in each relationship.

Our thoughts and words are always received by the Greater Consciousness of which we are an expression. God is not a cosmic bellhop responding to our every wish, but the energies we hold in thought, in heart, and in prayer contribute to the reality we experience. The focus of our own awareness always impacts and contributes to the Greater Awareness of which we are a part.

As part of this One, our choices and our actions have consequences. God may not be a big person who constantly watches and judges us, but the energies we carry and express affect our experience in the world. Our belief, thoughts, feelings, and actions have consequences because our energies are part of the whole.

God's blessing allows all existence to be: Allowing everything to be *is* the blessing. It is in that sense that you could say that God blesses everything. When we are open to the sacred life within us, we treat ourselves and others with greater respect and compassion. When we are closed to the awareness of this Greater Being, we experience separateness and fragmentation, get caught up in our ego issues, and our actions in the world express the separateness we experience. Energies of love support greater love; energies of hate support greater hate.

When we allow our own awareness to expand beyond our focus on our separate selves, we begin to breathe the more profound Love (the heart-space) and Being (the mind-space) that are our birthrights and at the foundations of our very nature. We are One in God. God is One in us. We each wear a face of God, and we reach out to each other with hands of God. In each moment, we are given responsibility for expressing the inclusivity of our shared existence through our words and through our actions. In a very real sense, God needs us all to do this. To remember, support, and celebrate our oneness while walking this journey as a separate human being is the work of *tikkun olam*, the completion of creation.

The scene at Mount Sinai, which is the quintessential moment of revelation in Jewish tradition, pictures the children of Israel standing together at the foot of the flaming, quaking, thundering mountain. We hear the blast of the shofar, the ram's horn, and are filled with awe and trembling. Moses translated the moment into the words known as the Ten Commandments, beginning:

> God spoke all these words, saying: I the LORD am your God who brought you out of the land of Egypt, the house of bondage; You shall have no other gods besides Me.
>
> *(Exodus 20:1–3)*

Jewish commentators through the ages have wondered what the people actually heard. Did everyone hear God speaking these Hebrew words? Some commentators suggest that we only heard the first Hebrew word, *Anokhi*, which means "I AM," and all the rest was translated to us through Moses. Others suggest that we only heard the very first syllable, which is "Ahhhh," like some universal chant of possibility. And yet others note that within the text itself, the only sound that is mentioned is the sound of the shofar. Perhaps that's what we heard, and Moses was sensitive enough to translate that sound into universal principles for spiritual growth as well as specific regulations for the survival of a community.

The sense of hearing is an internal matter, and we learn from the image of Sinai that we experience that ultimate communication on all perceptual and intuitive levels. We might hear a voice, almost always in our own language, feel a vibration, see images, and even taste and smell aspects of that perception. Since language is a function of the ego, our verbal translations of those greater moments are always inadequate attempts to express the realization itself.

Many years ago, I studied at the Esalen Institute with a teacher named John Lilly who was experimenting with sounds and the way the human brain creates meaning. A group of us lay on the floor as his sophisticated sound system played a tape loop of a three-syllable nonsense noise. At first, I lay there and heard nothing but gibberish. But, after a while, I began hearing first one word, then another. The longer I listened, the more sense the sounds made. Others had the same experience, but nobody heard the same words. Our individual minds automatically ordered the sounds we were hearing.

Later, we listened for an extended period to what was later defined as "pink noise." It sounded a little like a jet taking off. But as I listened, I began hearing an orchestra playing classical music behind the whooshing noise, with an acoustic guitar solo in the foreground. *I don't know this piece*, I remember thinking, *but it's beautiful. And it's amazing how bright the sound of the guitar is. I wonder how they did that in the recording.*

Well, it turned out that I was the only one who had an orchestra and a guitar—everyone "heard" something different in what was, quite simply, the rushing sound of pink noise. While I do not mean to say that the nonsense syllables and the pink noise reflect the sounds of revelation, it is instructive to recognize that people can perceive very different things when listening to the same sounds.

Perhaps everything that exists is an expression of the word of God, and we each hear according to the level of our listening. Some of us hear the messages of the oceans and the skies speaking the dangers of pollution. Some of us hear communications about the interconnectedness of all being. And others of us hear things that are not so inclusive.

It's as if there are various channels of communication, with some more restricted and some more open. Most of those who have received messages from the more universal sources have prepared for them through meditation and prayer so that they might be receptive. The spiritual teachers of humankind are translating a common vibration through their own particular traditions and cultures, so, as we have found, there is great similarity in their teachings.

But too often we become far more limiting and far more literal. I remember an interfaith gathering I attended several years ago in Southern California at which a minister held up her Bible and talked about the "word of God." After the program, I asked what she actually meant when she referenced the word of God. She again lifted her Bible, "This is the word of God," she said.

When I looked at her book, I noticed that it was the King James translation. I mentioned that this text was translated from the Latin that was translated from the Greek that was, in turn, translated from the Hebrew. Which did God say? The English? The Latin? The Greek? The Hebrew? She shook her head and took back her book. "*This* is the word of God," she said.

And this is where we have gotten ourselves into terrible trouble throughout history. When each of our traditions sees itself as the recipient of the only authorized words of God, we usually wind up defending our words against the words of others.

I don't believe that God speaks in words. Words are too small, too limiting, too particular, too separating.

Revelation is continual. It's in the very nature of existence and does not come into being one moment and disappear the next. It is we who are either open to that revelation or closed to it. The beautiful translations of that revelation that have come—and continue to come—through the great spiritual teachers of humankind are reflections of those moments when they opened to more universal vibrations. Each of those translations reminds us that we can open ourselves to the greater fullness of the Being we share.

The more inclusive the realization, the more loving the message, and the more compassionate the actions that follow, the more authentic the reception of authentic revelation.

Pastor Don's Reflections on God and Revelation

In Christianity, any discussion of God and revelation must begin with the fact that, traditionally, Jesus has been seen as *the* revelation of God. The word that is used to express that reality is *incarnation*. The life and teachings of Jesus gave material form to the substance of God. Everything about these topics has flowed from that conviction. In my experience, the centrality of Jesus leads me to the conviction that all people are called to try to understand how God is being made known to us.

It is startling, now that I think about it, that when I hear the word *God* today, I have the same reaction that I did when I was a small child. I see God as a masculine being up in the clouds. I don't know where that image came from, but I know many others who see God in the same way. Ironically, that is not the God I *believe* in. The God in my image from childhood is *out there* somewhere, looking down. And, even though I also believe that God transcends that sense of *out there*, it is possible for me to separate myself from God, to forget about God, to assume or to carry with me the sense that God is not always paying attention.

It is a good exercise to think about how our sense of God has changed over time. If it has changed, how has it changed and why?

Even though the word *God* still takes me to that familiar childhood image, as an adult I realize that no single image can embody that sense of Oneness that we three talk about. Rather than try to come up with one particular image, I now focus on articulating the feelings and the sensibilities that are stimulated by that sense of Oneness. Although this sensibility is essentially mystical, we approach it rationally, too, trying to understand something that cannot be captured fully in words or even in feelings. Poetry, music, and being together bring us much closer, but nothing ever gets us completely there.

Long before self-consciousness entered into the human experience, there existed the expression of the need to reconnect with nature, that deep desire to overcome the separation that happens at birth. I picture some lonely human being out on some lonely hillside on some ancient evening crying out to what he or she must have surely believed was "out there," with the hope of reconnecting, of becoming whole. It was a crying out, but it was also a kind of music, a recognition that mere words can hardly penetrate that great mystery of God. From this I extrapolate that we are indeed hardwired to long for the transcendence of the Divine. In mysticism, this is described as the great longing to be reconnected to the One after having been made into the many at creation.

When people in South Asia put their hands together and say to each other *namaste*, it means "the God in me greets the God in you." This suggests a different way of understanding God. It is far more difficult to forget something that lives in and around our beings rather than one whose home is in some far-off place called heaven.

In my tradition, we speak two truths with equal force: God is out there and God is in us. *Emmanuel*, one of the names given to Jesus, means "God with us." We bring that forward in the conveyance we call the Holy Spirit, the means by which God stays with us. Still, it is easy to keep God at arm's length. It is very easy to forget God, no matter how we conceive of the idea of God, until some need arises.

The writer of the book of the Acts of the Apostles speaks of "people of the way." This suggests both that the teachings of Jesus provided a path toward healing but also that we can help each other along the way. We are not alone. We have each other and we have God with us.

If the word *God* does point to something far deeper and more important than some image we formed as children, we must be consistent in our efforts to see and hear it. For example, we may take the phrase *God is love,* as a platitude, something to comfort us, to reassure us. But, in fact, this is the most important thing any human being could say about the Divine. Along with "God is one," and "God is compassionate," "God is love" actually defies the tendency to place God in some faraway realm, occasionally looking down and "answering" a prayer. If God is love, then we are never alone, because God could not be both *love* and *out there* somewhere. We are invited *in perpetuity* to pay attention to all those sights, sounds, thoughts, and actions that reflect the love that God is, or its absence, which calls us ever more deeply into making that love real in the world.

On the surface, a revelation is something that has been revealed, something that has been made known, has manifested. Theologically, a revelation is something that has been made known about God or about the relation between God and people. Aesthetically, a revelation is something that a work of art brings to the surface of human awareness. Art, some have said, is not the process of showing us new things. It is the process of showing us familiar things in new ways. Whichever we choose, the aesthetic dimension of revelation represents the mechanics underneath a circumstance of stunning importance.

Three questions inform the ways I approach the reality of revelation. How does God communicate with us? Has it changed over time? What exactly is our role in the process?

There was a time when people assumed that dreams and visions were messages from God to humanity. Dreams and visions are mysterious, so it isn't surprising that people would connect them with the mystery of God. But Thomas Aquinas, that famous Dominican, argued that that idea is inconsistent with the Aristotelian view of free will. In other words, how can we be free to make choices and at the same time, receive messages that deny such an ability to choose? Whether or not the ways God communicates with people have changed over time is still in debate. I would say that the human perception of how God communicates is still evolving. We are still trying to understand this. One important passage of scripture that informs my sense of this process appears in the Gospel according to Luke:

> As he came near and saw the city, he wept over it, saying, "If you, even you had only recognized on this day the things that make for peace! But now they are hidden from your eyes. Indeed, the days will come upon you, when your enemies will set up ramparts around you and surround you and hem you in on every side. They will crush you to the ground, you and your children within you, and they will not leave within you one stone upon another; because you did not recognize the time of your visitation from God.
>
> *(19:41–44)*

This is Jesus speaking from the Mount of Olives, overlooking the city of Jerusalem. He is making his way toward the city just before the annual observance of Passover and what for him will be his last week on earth, the week Christian people call Holy Week. While he is clearly speaking to Jerusalem, the message is much larger than that. Essentially, he is saying that the consequences of not being awake to the movements and actions of God are tragic.

One might see this passage as a reinforcement of Jesus's own divine status. But, as Ted and Jamal have taught me, no spiritual teacher would ever speak from a place of the ego, a place intended to strengthen or protect the role of the individual. That is why I like the last line of that passage as it appears in the *New English Bible*. It reads, "because you did not recognize God's moment when it came."[2] The difference might seem too subtle to justify any discussion, but the *New English Bible* deflects attention just a little more from Jesus and puts it more squarely on God.

At the same time, the verse presents another question: Does God speak to people in discreet moments, moments we might indeed miss? What, for example, if Moses had not been paying attention when God, speaking in the burning bush episode, urged him to go to Egypt and free the Hebrew people? This is a story that intends to tell us that God was revealed to Moses. More importantly, it conveys the reality that a message was received or, at least, was perceived to have been received.

We might ask the same question about the Christian story of Mary's visitation from the angels, giving her the divine message that she would bear a child to be named Jesus, whose life would be dedicated to bringing salvation and peace to the world. Was that a discrete message to her alone? If so, then revelation becomes far more egocentric than its cosmic value would suggest. So, what if God is "speaking" all the time and we, as individuals and as groups, occasionally get the message? Moses was paying attention. Mary was paying attention. What exactly is our role in revelation?

Clearly, we need to be paying attention, to be listening, to open our hearts and clear that sacred space for messages to be received. We do this through spiritual practice. The other component to revelation involves the human imagination, the ability to picture and sense things that either do not yet exist or of which we are yet ignorant. Our imaginations must be active in order to receive the messages that come under the heading of revelation. To keep our imaginations active, we must practice "making things up," using our creative energies to concretize ideas and communicate them to others. Having an active imagination is as important as spiritual practice because, in effect, they point in the same direction.

This still leaves me with the question: How do we know if an idea we have received is truly divine or simply a product of our imagination? I think we know the answer to that the same way we decide which verses, practices, or actions are consistent with the core teachings of our traditions and which ones are inconsistent. Such decisions can be made by individuals, but faith communities are necessary for the best and most fruitful processes of discernment.

Often, when I have an idea, I say that I have "been visited" or that it was the result of Providence—it was from God. I don't know that. But I believe it and I believe it because it makes sense for me to believe it. I strive to balance my subjective reality with objective thinking. It is a lifelong process and not one that is ever finally mastered or controlled.

Imam Jamal's Reflections on God and Revelation

Like millions of Muslims, I rhapsodize over a revelation, called *hadith qudsi*, that descended upon the Prophet Muhammad in a dream: "I was a secret Treasure and I longed to be known."[3] That secret Treasure, says the Qur'an, is both immanent and transcendent, both within us (*batin*) and without (*zahir*). To know the God within, we must do the inner work of removing what the Prophet Muhammad calls the "seventy thousand veils" between our ego and our divine Essence. To know the God without, we must offer ourselves in service to God's creation. And this, according to Islamic tradition, is the primary reason for our existence: to know, love, and serve God in this world so that we may walk with God on "spacious paths" for all eternity.

According to the Qur'an, our longing to know God was cosmically encoded in a primordial covenant when God gathered all the souls of unborn humanity and planted in us divine words in the form of a question: "Am I not your Sustainer?" In unison, we all testified, "Yes! Yes!" (7:172). When we arrive as individuals on earth, this cosmic memory is muted, and so the Qur'an pleads with us again and again, "Be conscious of God" and follows up with constant reminders: "What has seduced thee from thy Lord Most Beneficient?" (82:6) and "Do not barter away your bond with God for a trifling gain!" (16:95).

For all our longing and effort to truly know God, the Infinite One will always be a mystery to our human understanding. The Qur'an says that if all the trees in the universe were pens and the seven oceans were ink twice over, they would not be sufficient to describe the smallest fraction of the mysteries of God (31:27). Even so, Islamic tradition says that we can get a sense of God by meditating on the ninety-nine "beautiful names" mentioned in the Qur'an. By reflecting on these names, which are divine qualities, we may experience what mystics call a "glow of Presence."

The divine name mentioned most often in the Qur'an is Compassion—which, more than a divine quality, is the very essence of God. "Call upon Allah or call upon the All Merciful" (17:110), says the Qur'an. The Holy Book promises, "Say: O my servants who have transgressed against their souls! Despair not of the Mercy of God: for God forgives all sins; for God is Oft-Forgiving, Most Merciful" (39:53). Such is the compassion of God, said the Prophet, that if you take one step toward God, God takes seven toward you; walk toward God and God comes running. Mystics exclaim that not only do the thirsty seek water, water seeks the thirsty.

We humans, with our imperfect understanding, often wonder how it is that a compassionate God could allow such terrible things as genocide and natural disasters to occur, causing untold suffering and pain to countless innocent people. No one can explain such a mystery. But there is an aspect to this mystery that amazes me. In my ministry I have counseled people who were so furious at God— because of some disaster in their lives—that they expressly insisted I make no mention of God. But as they have worked to recover from trauma and heal their pain, all these people have transformed their rage toward God and become passionate devotees of God. That, to me, is the greater mystery.

It seems to me that God wants us to grow in faith, and that we have to make continuous efforts to fulfill the dizzying honors and responsibilities God has bestowed upon us. Divinity has exalted us by placing upon us the *Amanah* (33:72), or "trust" of awareness and free will. All of humanity has been appointed as vice-regents of God on earth. The Qur'an warns us, "Do not sow corruption on earth," and laments that "corruption has appeared on the land and in the sea because of what the hands of humans have wrought" (30:41). God will help us, but we have to strive constantly to grow in awareness and build a just and equitable society. There is a popular saying in Western culture that God helps those who help themselves. The Muslim version of this saying is told in the story about a Bedouin who asked Muhammad if he should tie his camel to a post while he went into the mosque to pray, or whether he should trust in God alone to keep the camel safe. The Prophet replied, "First tie the camel to the post, then trust in God."

The Islamic belief in the oneness of God is very clearly stated in the Qur'an: "He is God, the One and Only; God, the Eternal, Absolute; He begetteth not, nor is He begotten; and there is none like unto Him" (112:1–4). There is no room for equivocation in this statement of belief, but if our understanding of God is based simply on parroting the words, we run the risk of making superficial distinctions between "my God" and "your God." Ignorance turns into arrogance, and soon we regard those who don't subscribe to every word of our particular creed as blasphemers, idolaters, or unbelievers. Rather than judging the quality of others' beliefs, we need to look at our own.

The Qur'an categorizes three stages of belief and asks us to build faith and advance in consciousness by moving through those three stages. Most of us are stuck in the first stage, which is belief based on hearsay. The second stage is based on personal insight and witnessing, and the last stage emerges through a personal experience of inner certainty (102:5, 102:7, and 69:51). It is telling that all Islamic sages who have transformed hearsay belief into experiential faith have ultimately achieved an inner spaciousness that is inclusive of all religions. Beyond the forms of trinity and gods and goddesses is the same one God. The nirvana of Buddhism is the same as God, and both atheists and agnostics simply call God by a different name: justice, humanity, compassion. To Muslims who adamantly and arrogantly insist that their belief about God is the only correct one and criticize non-Muslim ideas of Divinity, Rumi exclaims: "You say you have seen Him, but your eyes are two stones. You say you have known Him, but nothing in you trembles. You still say 'I' when you speak of surviving His glory: No one who has seen It has ever survived."[4]

Spiritual masters remark that if we take to heart the verse that says "Everywhere you turn is the Face of Allah," then even the devil is the face of God. When Satan promised to waylay humanity, he invoked the power and glory of God: "By Thy power, I will put them all in the wrong" (38:82). The presence of Satan, called the "slinking whisperer" in the Qur'an, serves the necessary purpose of challenging us to strengthen our moral fiber. By the same token, angels also are the face of God, and their energies exist to strengthen our power to make good choices. Thus, both angels and devils are part of the mystery of God.

If the Face of Allah is everywhere, it behooves us to spend less time and energy on trying to "understand" God and more time living in a way that expands our awareness of God in every face we meet. The fourteenth-century poet Hafiz said that God had told him a sublime secret: "Each soul," God said to him, "each soul completes Me."

Islamic tradition holds that not only are the revelations in the Qur'an divinely inspired, they are the actual words of God in Arabic. The revelations in the Qur'an are directly linked to the Prophet Muhammad, who even as a child spent long periods in silent reflection. At the age of forty, in 610 CE, Muhammad was meditating late one night in a Meccan cave when a blinding light appeared, announced itself as the angel Gabriel, and commanded him to "Recite." In a scene reminiscent of the prophet Moses's encounter with the burning bush, Muhammad tremblingly replied, "I am not one of those who recite." But the angel persisted and squeezed him painfully. Petrified with fear that he was losing his mind, Muhammad fled the mountain, but later he returned and once again encountered the mysterious light. Again he felt the force of an invisible grip, and this time from the depths of his being, he uttered words of exquisite beauty, which were seared into his soul. It is not surprising that the revelations caused the Prophet so much physical distress. The words of God are weighty and awesome, says the Qur'an. Had the words been bestowed upon a mountain, the mountain would have "cleave[d] asunder for awe of God" (59:21).

This mysterious transmission from God to the angel Gabriel to the Prophet Muhammad occurred intermittently for twenty-three years. The collection of these words constitutes the Qur'an, which means "Recitation." The recitations cover a vast range of topics, including spiritual guidance and discernment, remembrance, and a compendium of social rules and regulations. By the end of the seventh century, a consistent version of the 114 chapters of the Qur'an in written form was produced with diacritics to indicate the correct pronunciation of each word.

All scholars of Arabic agree that the language of the Qur'an is unsurpassed in its literary beauty. Because of the limitations of human language, it is as if the entire musical scale is being expressed through one note. Thus, the revelations have unique rhythms, impassioned cadences, dramatic rumblings, and mysterious oaths and adjurations. The vibrations of the verses penetrate the Muslim body and soul even before they reach the mind. As a child I loved to recite the verses because I was told that God hides in the verses so that, as you recite them, God can kiss your lips.

I always wondered how God spoke to Muhammad. In a famous traditional story, the Prophet explained that at the onset of a revelation, he typically heard the sound of chimes, felt as if his soul was being torn from him, and through this sound, "I have understood what God meant to say." In other words, the sound eventually transformed itself into different words. To explain what it means by revelation, the Qur'an mentions "sending down" (*tanzil*) and "inspiration" (*wahy*). The Holy Book explains that revelation unfolds when "trustworthy divine inspiration has alighted with it from on high upon thy heart" (26:193–194).

Prophets are not infallible. According to early biographers, in a controversial and disputed incident, Muhammad told a Meccan crowd about a revelation that accepted three of their favorite goddess idols as intercessors, whereupon the crowd roared in approval and bowed to him. That evening, the angel Gabriel chastised Muhammad for listening to the whispers of Satan. In an extraordinary display of courage and faith, the Prophet publicly retracted the previous revelation, thus earning the abiding wrath and persecution of the community. God reassured Muhammad in another revelation that it is the lot of every prophet and messenger to have the devil interfere with divine revelations, but "God will cancel anything [vain] that Satan throws in, and God will confirm [and establish] His Signs" (22:52). Prophets are fallible but no mistake is left uncorrected by God.

The Qur'an itself reminds us that the words of God have several layers of meaning and that every verse has an "inner" and an "outer" layer. Some verses are literal and others, metaphorical. Ultimately, it is only through knowledge of the heart that we truly understand. The Qur'an reveals its secrets to "everyone whose heart is wide awake—that is, [everyone who] lends ears with a conscious mind" (50:37). Muslims meticulously refrain from criticizing any Qur'anic verses, even those that seem on the surface to be "un-Qur'anic," but will interpret the meanings of problematic verses in various ways. Given today's political climate, in which many Muslims feel that Islam is under attack by critics in the West, some countries, such as Pakistan and Saudi Arabia, go to absurd lengths to "protect" the Qur'an by legislating severe penalties, even death, for someone who criticizes the Holy Book. Islamic sages counter this sense of insecurity through a simple teaching: If you spit at the majesty of the sky, does this pollute the sky? Of course not—in fact, the spit returns to your own eye!

Over the centuries, Islamic teachers have lamented that we humans prefer to argue endlessly about the exact meaning of a divine revelation, rather than live the spirit of its message. Rumi said of his lifelong study of the Qur'an, "I have taken the marrow from the Qur'an and thrown the bones to the dogs." This is not meant to be disrespectful but to convey a teaching. Let us take the essential message of the revelation to heart and let the theologians quibble about the dry-bone technicalities.

Several non-Muslims in my community have studied the Qur'an for extended periods and have found that there is literally "something for everyone" in the Holy Book. Christians are usually surprised and delighted to find that Islamic revelations talk of the virgin birth of Jesus and that an entire chapter is devoted to Mary. Jews feel resonances with the repeated emphasis on the oneness of God and the passion for justice: "Be just; this is closest to God consciousness" (5:8). Hindus see their religion echoed in the verse "Everywhere you turn is the Face of Allah" (2:115), and Buddhists find the idea of impermanence beautifully articulated in the words: "All that is on earth will perish: but will abide [forever] the Face of thy Lord—full of Majesty, Bounty, and Honor" (55:26–27). Activists are impressed by the Qur'an's insistence that what ensures passage to heaven is neither gender nor religion but primarily doing "righteous deeds" (49:13, 5:69). Environmentalists deeply appreciate the verse: "Assuredly, the creation of the heavens and the earth is a greater [matter] than the creation of men, yet most men understand not" (40:57).

My parents told me that Rumi said, "The Qur'an is like a shy bride. Don't approach her directly. Approach her through her friends." I usually advise those interested in the Holy Book not to rush out and buy a copy of the Qur'an. First, study a book that contains selected verses with commentary, then connect with one of the many mystics who abound in Islam, such as Ibn Arabi, Rumi, and Hafiz. Only then will your heart and mind be ready to read the Qur'an with real understanding.

Concluding Comments

Translation is always an approximation, even when we are translating between languages that have a common root. English is far removed from Hebrew, Aramaic, and Arabic, and today's English is far removed from its Greek ancestor. And when the original texts are thousands of years removed from us, the challenges of translation multiply. Surely the many translations of all our sacred texts reflects the difficulty of grasping exactly what was being expressed.

So we strive to achieve the most authentic approximation possible and learn from the teachers over the centuries with whose striving we identify. We know that our own beliefs evolve as our understanding and experience grow. What we have presented reflects, as best we know how, where we are now. We strive to remain open to the next steps in our own spiritual evolution and hope that you do, too.

Ultimately, we are guided by our understanding of the core teachings of our traditions. Just as they allow us to evaluate consistent and inconsistent aspects of our traditions, they allow us, as well, to better appreciate our texts and our shared quest to celebrate the Universal.

No matter what our differences, we believe there is a connection between the Universe and us. Whenever that connection is forged, words of teaching appear. They will be translated through the ones who are most willing and able to hear.

Conclusion

Going Astray toward Greater Meaning

Religions go astray when they contribute more to human suffering than they do to human healing. We go astray as individuals when we forget the essential nature of our being and identify only with the things we have and the things we do. We become human *doings* and human *havings* rather than human *beings*, and the consequences are greater separateness, conflict, and hopelessness.

Within the five stages of interfaith dialogue, spelled out in the Introduction, the key to understanding the ways in which our religious institutions go astray is contained in the third stage—sharing consistencies and inconsistencies within our traditions. As we named the parts of our own paths that were difficult for us, we discovered how our institutions—and how *all* institutions—go astray. And we began to acknowledge the consequences of this drifting. What is crucial, however, is the examination of the purpose of going astray. If our institutions go astray, and if we as individuals go astray, perhaps there is meaning in this straying.

We Go Astray in Order to Grow

We used to think that our going astray was a terrible mistake. When we as individuals forget the deeper realities of our being, and we as institutions neglect the spiritual principles that give our lives greater meaning, we miss the mark, and we can do great harm. But if it is our *nature* to go astray, perhaps it is both a mistake and an opportunity.

To get from the experience of the mistake to the awareness of the opportunity requires both taking responsibility for the mistake and accepting forgiveness. Acknowledging responsibility often encourages us to feel bad about ourselves and what we've done; it can reinforce our sense that we are bad people. But our mistakes are *doings* and *havings,* not *beings*. We can *do* evil, we can *have* evil, but we cannot *be* evil. Once we realize this, we can forgive ourselves and forgive others. Then, and only then, can we open to the opportunities for growth revealed through our mistakes. Forgiveness releases us from needing the past to be anything other than it was and allows us to step into our true nature.

We believe that our going astray is purposeful. As individuals, we sometimes forget that which gives us greater purpose and meaning in order to experience the absolute joy of self-remembering. When we become unconscious to the deeper nature of our being, collapsing into an identity delineated by what we do and what we have, we have the opportunity to awaken at a fuller level of awareness. Perhaps you have experienced this in the context of your primary relationships. When we forget, we take the other person for granted, becoming unconscious to the wonder and the immediacy of a loving relationship. But if we perceive this unconsciousness simply to be one of the natural rhythms of our existence, and not blame ourselves for it, we can draw ourselves again into the preciousness of the moment. Again and again, then, we can awaken to celebrate even more deeply the people who are in our lives. Our forgetting can lead us to an even greater remembering.

As institutions, going astray is the way we participate in the ongoing process of our evolution. It is simply the nature of institutions to get caught up in maintaining what has been created. Our institutions naturally resist change, which is perceived as threatening to their continuity. This resistance to change is often expressed through the very issues that we have identified in chapters 1–4: Our institutions proclaim exclusive ownership of Truth, they respond violently to enforce conformity, they support the status quo in the unequal power accorded to men and women, and they defend particular views of what constitutes an authentic loving relationship.

When we dare to share our institutional strayings, we open our institutions to advance their own evolution. How can we think that evolution has stopped? It is the very nature of the spiritual quest to provide ever-deepening levels of awakening. There is the tendency, often promoted by institutions fearing change, to imagine that the ancients were far more spiritually developed than we are. While acknowledging the profound teachings of the past, can we not imagine that there is more yet to unfold? In spirituality, as in science, we are always at the frontier of discovering what we have not yet realized about the nature of reality.

And this is our response to those who seek the end of faith rather than the evolution of faith. The very failings that some would use to condemn the Abrahamic traditions can serve as the foundation for renewal. This is the possibility of a radical renaissance of spirit through the transcending wisdom of our heritage.

An Invitation to Personal and Institutional Evolution

We have been pursuing interfaith dialogue in order to realize a foundation that can support greater collaboration toward healing the significant challenges of our time. Now we understand that there is another purpose to this exploration of dialogue: becoming available for the evolution of human *being*. We believe that awakening to the more spiritual dimensions of our being allows us to be more available than ever to engage in our shared evolution.

And this is where the story can get even more interesting. Interfaith dialogue can go beyond faith, helping us in any situation in which we have serious difficulty talking and listening to each other—even politics. We are not in favor of challenging the separation of religion and state—in fact, we are supportive of that separation. But the techniques of interfaith dialogue provide us with the most effective ways of transcending the political polarities that have been strangling our capacities to deal with the pressing issues of our day.

Religious institutions provide a foundation and a context for nourishing our souls with spiritual wisdom. But that very spiritual wisdom challenges us to walk those teachings into our world. Our political structure provides the context for that walking. How can we utilize spiritual teaching to help us heal our world? We understand this now to be the evolution of our own work in interfaith dialogue. This may even be the focus of our next book.

What You Can Do Now

Now that you have had the opportunity to hear our stories, to read about the core teachings of our traditions, and to discover some of the particular beauty and some of the particular awkwardness in each of our faiths, we hope that you will be interested in deepening interfaith relationships for yourself. Whether or not you are a member of a faith community, we all seek meaning and purpose in life. The different ways in which we seek meaning can be the source of incredible vitality and energy as we awaken to the magnificence of the diversity of humanity. Each of us brings rich diversity to the experience of living now on this planet.

One of the groups we had the privilege of meeting during the years of our traveling is the Interfaith Ministries for Greater Houston. They introduced us to the Amazing Faiths Dinner Dialogue Project which they cofounded with the Boniuk Center for the Study and Advancement of Religious Tolerance at Rice University. They have developed a series of questions to encourage interfaith conversations. They suggest that each question be printed on a separate card, so that as people go around a circle, each person picks a different question, reads it aloud, and then responds. You can find the list of questions relating to religious and spiritual experiences on our website (www.interfaithamigos.com). This is one of the clearest ways we have found to provide rich opportunities to listen with an open heart to another person's experience. Dialogue groups like this allow us to meet our neighbors and coworkers, friends, and, yes, even relatives, in precious ways. Sharing our stories provides the context to counteract the fears that we all share.

The United Religions Initiative (uri.org) creates interfaith cooperative circles for people to join together and cooperate in projects of earth care and social justice. URI is a resource for information about forming such groups in your community. The Charter for Compassion (charterforcompassion.org) provides resources for promoting more compassionate action in our cities.

We encourage you to advocate for religious literacy education in your local public schools. This is a way to help our children develop appreciative understandings of the traditions of others. We have found material by Diane L. Moore, who teaches at Harvard Divinity School, to be of great help in explaining how classes in religious literacy can be created.

Finally, we encourage you to establish patterns and habits in your life that permit you to implement spiritual practices, such as meditation, prayer, journaling, and the study of sacred texts. For more on that topic we invite you to see our first book, *Getting to the Heart of Interfaith: The Eye-Opening, Hope-Filled Friendship of a Pastor, a Rabbi and a Sheikh.*[1] Spiritual practices help us to discover and evolve our spiritual center as we grow and become more open to the gifts that others bring to our lives.

One of the ways we discover oneness is through singing together. We have created a theme song that we use to conclude our presentations. The words of "Oneness" include Arabic, Hebrew, and English:

Bismillah ir Rahman ir Rahim,
In the Name of God, boundlessly
Compassionate and Merciful
La ilaha illa Allah hu.
There is no god but God.
Adonai hu ha-Elohim hu,
The Transcendent One awakens within each of
us as our God.
It's all one and I AM as I AM.
It's all one and I AM as I AM.

In singing together, we celebrate the Being we share and are recalled to meaning and purpose. May our sharing and our singing support the healing we all need.

Acknowledgments

From Pastor Don, Rabbi Ted, and Imam Jamal

We wish to express our deep gratitude to Ruth Neuwald Falcon, our communications director, and to Mitchell Fink, our publicist. Their continuing efforts have supported the expansion of our work in very significant ways. Our gratitude for Third Place Commons in Lake Forest Park, Washington, which provides us with such a warm and inviting setting where we plan, write, read to each other, and where, on occasion, we relax together. Special thanks to Marcus Borg and to James Forbes, two men whose commitment to the spiritual essence of their traditions is a continuing inspiration. We are grateful for their support and their encouragement. We want to acknowledge our friends at *Yes! Magazine* for publishing our blog and allowing us to share their passion for economic justice.

We are especially grateful for the kindness and expertise of Emily Wichland, vice president of Editorial and Production at SkyLight Paths Publishing, for her encouragement and her help with this project. Our thanks to Alys Yablon Wylen for her editing skills. She helped keep us on track when we wandered and made sure our book said what we meant.

Acknowledgments from Pastor Don

I wish to thank my family—my wife, Judy; our daughters, Mary and Alice; and my parents. I also want to express appreciation to those who have been mentors to me: Arthur Adams, Donald R. Purkey, G. Robert Jacks, Nicholas Van Dyck, Wallace Alston, David Korten, Avery Post, Frank Kelsey, Edward Wenk, Jr., Lloyd Averill, and Mary Hooker.

Acknowledgments from Rabbi Ted

Although she is communications director for all of us, I want to express my gratitude for the continuing support and wise counsel of Ruth Neuwald Falcon, who is also my wife. Her editing and writing skills have added significantly to this book. I am, as always, grateful to my teachers and my students who continue to help me learn and to three unique mentors: Reverend Clifton King, Rabbi Michael Roth, and Arthur L. Kovacs, PhD.

Acknowledgments from Imam Jamal

I wish to express deep gratitude for three circles of love in my life. My first circle consists of my beloved late parents, Ataur and Suraiya Rahman. The second comprises my precious family: daughter Kristina, brother Kamal, sister Aysu, and my loving relatives, Naz, Diran, Esha, Neal, Emana, Ataur, Suraiya, Ummul, Javed, Nuzhat, Sufiara, Ismet, Ishtiaque, Ripa, Ashu, and Tanvir. My third circle includes my lifelong friends: Reverend Karen Lindquist, Katayoon Naficy, Sally Jo de Vargas, Linda Jo Pym, and Faren Bachelis. Special thanks to Kate Elias, whose help in shaping and editing my pieces was invaluable, and to friends and colleagues from my classes and Interfaith Community Church, whose love for learning and commitment to expanding mind and heart have made me a more complete Muslim.

Notes

Chapter 1

1. Wallace Alston, *The Church* (Atlanta: John Knox Press, 1984), 15.
2. Amin Maalouf, *The Crusades through Arab Eyes* (New York: Schocken, 1989).
3. Adolf Hitler, *Mein Kampf*, complete and unabridged fully annotated, ed. John Chamberlain and Sidney B. Fay, et al. (New York: Reynal & Hitchcock/Houghton Mifflin Company, 1939), 84.
4. Robert Bly, *The Kabir Book: Forty-Four of the Ecstatic Poems of Kabir* (Boston: Beacon Press, 2007), 55.
5. Hadith Collection of Bukhari.
6. Ibid.

Chapter 2

1. Louis de Bernières, *Birds without Wings* (New York: Alfred A. Knopf, 2004).
2. Walter Wink, *The Powers That Be* (New York: Doubleday, 1999).

Chapter 3

1. St. Thomas Aquinas, *Summa Theologica,* Complete English Edition in Five Volumes. Trans. by Fathers of the English Dominican Province (Notre Dame, IN: Ave Maria Press, 1948), ST Ia, Q. 92, A. 1, ad 1.
2. Abul Ala Maududi, *Towards Understanding the Quran* (New Delhi, India: Markazi Maktaba Islami Publishers, 2006).
3. Yusuf Ali, *The Meaning of the Holy Qur'an* (Bettsville, MD: Amana Publications, 1989).
4. A. Nooruddin, A. R. Omar, and A. M. Omar, *The Holy Qur'an* (Noor Foundation International, 1991); www.IslamUSA.org.
5. Hadith collection of Abu Dawud and others.
6. Tafsir al-Mizan by al-Tabataba'i.
7. Muhammad Asad, *The Message of the Quran* (Bath, England: The Book Foundation, 2003), 60, n211.

8. Hadith collection of Bukhari.
9. John Esposito and Dalia Mogahed, *Who Speaks for Islam? What a Billion Muslims Really Think* (New York: Gallup Press, 2007), 116.
10. Pinar Ilkkaracan, ed., *Women and Sexuality in Muslim Societies* (Istanbul: Women for Women's Human Rights, 2000), 333.
11. "Fatwa: Open letter to Darul Uloom Deoband from Bharatiya Muslim Mahila Andalon," in *Indian Express and Indian Muslim Observer*, November 26, 2010; www.indianmuslimobserver.com/2010/11fatwa-open-letter-to-darul-uloom.htm.

Chapter 4

1. Hadith collection of Tabarani.
2. Hadith collection of Abu Dawud and Tirmidhi.
3. Yusuf al-Qaradawi, quoted in "Livingstone Lauds the Man Who Defends the Killing of Gays," Jenny McCartney, *The Telegraph*, July 11, 2004.
4. Tariq Ramadan, *Islam and Homosexuality*, www.tariqramadan.com, posted May 29, 2009.
5. Robert Putnam and David Campbell, *American Grace: How Religion Divides and Unites Us* (New York: Simon & Schuster, 2010).
6. Robert Wright, "Islamophobia and Homophobia," *New York Times*, October 26, 2010.

Chapter 5

1. David Cooper, *God Is a Verb: Kabbalah and the Practice of Mystical Judaism* (New York: Riverhead Books, 1998).
2. *New English Bible* (New York: Oxford University Press, 1970).
3. Javad Nurbakhsh, *Traditions of the Prophet* (New York: Khaniqahi Nimatullahi Publications, 1981), 13, 56.
4. Andrew Harvey, trans., 365-Day Online Course, "A Year of Rumi," lesson 44; www.intent.com/dailyom/blog/online-course-year-rumi-andrew-harvey.

Conclusion

1. Don Mackenzie, Ted Falcon, and Jamal Rahman, *Getting to the Heart of Interfaith: The Eye-Opening, Hope-Filled Friendship of a Pastor, a Rabbi and a Sheikh* (Woodstock, VT: SkyLight Paths, 2009).

Suggestions for Further Reading

Further Readings in Judaism

Comins, Mike. *Making Prayer Real: Leading Jewish Spiritual Voices on Why Prayer Is Difficult and What to Do About It.* Woodstock, VT: Jewish Lights Publishing, 2010.

Falcon, Rabbi Ted, PhD, and David Blatner. *Judaism For Dummies.* Hoboken, NJ: Wiley, 2001.

Kula, Irwin, and Vanessa L. Ochs, PhD, eds. *The Book of Jewish Sacred Practices: Clal's Guide to Everyday and Holiday Rituals and Blessings.* Woodstock, VT: Jewish Lights Publishing, 2001.

Steinberg, Milton. *Basic Judaism.* New York: Mariner Books, 1965.

Further Readings in Christianity

Alston, Wallace M. Jr. *The Church.* Atlanta: John Knox Press, 1984.

Borg, Marcus J. *Jesus: Uncovering the Life, Teachings, and Relevance of a Religious Revolutionary.* New York: HarperCollins, 2006.

Butler Bass, Diana. *A People's History of Christianity: The Other Side of the Story.* New York: HarperCollins, 2009.

Cox, Harvey J. Jr. *The Future of Faith.* New York: HarperCollins, 2009.

Forbes, James A. Jr. *Whose Gospel? A Concise Guide to Progressive Protestantism.* New York: The New Press, 2010.

Freemantle, Anne, ed. *The Protestant Mystics.* Boston: Little, Brown and Company, 1964.

Nouwen, Henri, Michael J. Christensen, and Rebecca J. Laird. *Spiritual Formation: Following the Movements of the Spirit.* New York: HarperCollins, 2010.

Pagels, Elaine. *The Gnostic Gospels.* New York: Vintage Books, 1979.

———. *Beyond Belief.* New York: Vintage Books, 2003.

Wink, Walter, *Homosexuality and Christian Faith.* Minneapolis: Fortress Press, 1999.

Further Readings in Islam

Abou El Fadl, Khaled. *The Place of Tolerance in Islam.* Boston: Beacon Press, 2002.

Aslan, Reza. *No god but God: The Origins, Evolution, and Future of Islam.* New York: Random House, 2006.

Esposito, John and Dalia Mogahed. *Who Speaks for Islam? What a Billion Muslims Really Think.* New York: Gallup Press, 2007.

Hazleton, Lesley. *After the Prophet.* New York: Doubleday, 2009.

Rahman, Jamal. *The Fragrance of Faith: The Enlightened Heart of Islam.* Bath, England: The Book Foundation, 2004.

Rahman, Jamal, Kathleen Elias, and Ann Redding. *Out of Darkness into Light: Spiritual Guidance in the Quran with Reflections from Christian and Jewish Sources.* New York: Morehouse Publishing, 2009.

Wadud, Amina. *Quran and Women: Re-reading the Sacred Text from a Woman's Perspective.* New York: Oxford University Press, 1999.

Further Readings in Interfaith

Abu-Nimer, Mohammed, Emily Welty, and Amal I. Khoury. *Unity in Diversity: Interfaith Dialogue in the Middle East.* Washington, D.C.: United States Institute of Peace Press, 2007.

Byrne, Máire. *The Names of God in Judaism, Christianity, and Islam: A Basis for Interfaith Dialogue.* London and New York: Continuum, 2011.

Harkins, Franklin T., ed. *Transforming Relations: Essays on Jews and Christians throughout History in Honor of Michael A. Signer.* South Bend, IN: University of Notre Dame Press, 2010.

Mackenzie, Pastor Don, Rabbi Ted Falcon, and Sheikh Jamal Rahman. *Getting to the Heart of Interfaith: The Eye-Opening, Hope-Filled Friendship of a Pastor, a Rabbi and a Sheikh.* Woodstock, VT: SkyLight Paths Publishing, 2009.

McCarthy, Kate. *Interfaith Encounters in America.* New Brunswick, NJ: Rutgers University Press, 2007.

Niebuhr, Gustav, *Beyond Tolerance: Searching for Interfaith Understanding in America.* New York: Viking, 2008.

Inspiration

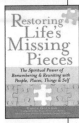

Restoring Life's Missing Pieces
The Spiritual Power of Remembering & Reuniting with People, Places, Things & Self
by Caren Goldman
A powerful and thought-provoking look at reunions of all kinds as roads to remembering and re-membering ourselves.
6 x 9, 208 pp, Quality PB, 978-1-59473-295-9 **$16.99**

How Did I Get to Be 70 When I'm 35 Inside?
Spiritual Surprises of Later Life
by Linda Douty
Encourages you to focus on the inner changes of aging to help you greet your later years as the grand adventure they can be.
6 x 9, 208 pp, Quality PB, 978-1-59473-297-3 **$16.99**

Spiritually Healthy Divorce: Navigating Disruption with Insight & Hope
by Carolyne Call
A spiritual map to help you move through the twists and turns of divorce.
6 x 9, 224 pp, Quality PB, 978-1-59473-288-1 **$16.99**

Who Is My God? 2nd Edition
An Innovative Guide to Finding Your Spiritual Identity
by the Editors at SkyLight Paths
Provides the Spiritual Identity Self-Test™ to uncover the components of your unique spirituality.
6 x 9, 160 pp, Quality PB, 978-1-59473-014-6 **$15.99**

God the What?
What Our Metaphors for God Reveal about Our Beliefs in God
by Carolyn Jane Bohler
Inspires you to consider a wide range of images of God in order to refine how you imagine God.
6 x 9, 192 pp, Quality PB, 978-1-59473-251-5 **$16.99**

Journeys of Simplicity
Traveling Light with Thomas Merton, Bashō, Edward Abbey, Annie Dillard & Others
by Philip Harnden
Invites you to consider a more graceful way of traveling through life. PB includes journal pages to help you get started on your own spiritual journey.
5 x 7¼, 144 pp, Quality PB, 978-1-59473-181-5 **$12.99**
5 x 7¼, 128 pp, HC, 978-1-893361-76-8 **$16.95**

Or phone, fax, mail or e-mail to: SKYLIGHT PATHS Publishing
Sunset Farm Offices, Route 4 • P.O. Box 237 • Woodstock, Vermont 05091
Tel: (802) 457-4000 • Fax: (802) 457-4004 • www.skylightpaths.com
Credit card orders: (800) 962-4544 (8:30AM–5:30PM ET Monday–Friday)
Generous discounts on quantity orders. SATISFACTION GUARANTEED. Prices subject to change.

Sacred Texts—SkyLight Illuminations Series

Offers today's spiritual seeker an enjoyable entry into the great classic texts of the world's spiritual traditions. Each classic is presented in an accessible translation, with facing pages of guided commentary from experts, giving you the keys you need to understand the history, context and meaning of the text.

CHRISTIANITY

Celtic Christian Spirituality: Essential Writings—Annotated & Explained
Annotation by Mary C. Earle; Foreword by John Philip Newell
Explores how the writings of this lively tradition embody the gospel.
5½ x 8½, 176 pp, Quality PB, 978-1-59473-302-4 **$16.99**

The End of Days: Essential Selections from Apocalyptic Texts— Annotated & Explained *Annotation by Robert G. Clouse, PhD*
Helps you understand the complex Christian visions of the end of the world.
5½ x 8½, 224 pp, Quality PB, 978-1-59473-170-9 **$16.99**

The Hidden Gospel of Matthew: Annotated & Explained
Translation & Annotation by Ron Miller Discover the words and events that have the strongest connection to the historical Jesus.
5½ x 8½, 272 pp, Quality PB, 978-1-59473-038-2 **$16.99**

The Infancy Gospels of Jesus: Apocryphal Tales from the Childhoods of Mary and Jesus—Annotated & Explained
Translation & Annotation by Stevan Davies; Foreword by A. Edward Siecienski, PhD
A startling presentation of the early lives of Mary, Jesus and other biblical figures that will amuse and surprise you. 5½ x 8½, 176 pp, Quality PB, 978-1-59473-258-4 **$16.99**

The Lost Sayings of Jesus: Teachings from Ancient Christian, Jewish, Gnostic and Islamic Sources—Annotated & Explained
Translation & Annotation by Andrew Phillip Smith; Foreword by Stephan A. Hoeller
This collection of more than three hundred sayings depicts Jesus as a Wisdom teacher who speaks to people of all faiths as a mystic and spiritual master.
5½ x 8½, 240 pp, Quality PB, 978-1-59473-172-3 **$16.99**

Philokalia: The Eastern Christian Spiritual Texts—Selections Annotated & Explained *Annotation by Allyne Smith; Translation by G. E. H. Palmer, Phillip Sherrard and Bishop Kallistos Ware*
The first approachable introduction to the wisdom of the Philokalia, the classic text of Eastern Christian spirituality. 5½ x 8½, 240 pp, Quality PB, 978-1-59473-103-7 **$16.99**

The Sacred Writings of Paul: Selections Annotated & Explained
Translation & Annotation by Ron Miller Leads you into the exciting immediacy of Paul's teachings. 5½ x 8½, 224 pp, Quality PB, 978-1-59473-213-3 **$16.99**

Saint Augustine of Hippo: Selections from *Confessions* and Other Essential Writings—Annotated & Explained
Annotation by Joseph T. Kelley, PhD; Translation by the Augustinian Heritage Institute
Provides insight into the mind and heart of this foundational Christian figure.
5½ x 8½, 272 pp, Quality PB, 978-1-59473-282-9 **$16.99**

St. Ignatius Loyola—The Spiritual Writings: Selections Annotated & Explained *Annotation by Mark Mossa, SJ*
Draws from contemporary translations of original texts focusing on the practical mysticism of Ignatius of Loyola. 5½ x 8½, 224 pp (est), Quality PB, 978-1-59473-301-7 **$16.99**

Sex Texts from the Bible: Selections Annotated & Explained
Translation & Annotation by Teresa J. Hornsby; Foreword by Amy-Jill Levine
Demystifies the Bible's ideas on gender roles, marriage, sexual orientation, virginity, lust and sexual pleasure. 5½ x 8½, 208 pp, Quality PB, 978-1-59473-217-1 **$16.99**

Sacred Texts—continued

CHRISTIANITY—continued

Spiritual Writings on Mary: Annotated & Explained
Annotation by Mary Ford-Grabowsky; Foreword by Andrew Harvey
Examines the role of Mary, the mother of Jesus, as a source of inspiration in
history and in life today. 5½ x 8½, 288 pp, Quality PB, 978-1-59473-001-6 **$16.99**

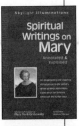

The Way of a Pilgrim: The Jesus Prayer Journey—Annotated & Explained
Translation & Annotation by Gleb Pokrovsky; Foreword by Andrew Harvey
A classic of Russian Orthodox spirituality.
5½ x 8½, 160 pp, Illus., Quality PB, 978-1-893361-31-7 **$14.95**

GNOSTICISM

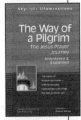

Gnostic Writings on the Soul: Annotated & Explained
Translation & Annotation by Andrew Phillip Smith; Foreword by Stephan A. Hoeller
Reveals the inspiring ways your soul can remember and return to its unique,
divine purpose. 5½ x 8½, 144 pp, Quality PB, 978-1-59473-220-1 **$16.99**

The Gospel of Philip: Annotated & Explained
Translation & Annotation by Andrew Phillip Smith; Foreword by Stevan Davies
Reveals otherwise unrecorded sayings of Jesus and fragments of Gnostic mythology.
5½ x 8½, 160 pp, Quality PB, 978-1-59473-111-2 **$16.99**

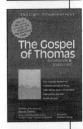

The Gospel of Thomas: Annotated & Explained
Translation & Annotation by Stevan Davies; Foreword by Andrew Harvey
Sheds new light on the origins of Christianity and portrays Jesus as a wisdom-loving sage.
5½ x 8½, 192 pp, Quality PB, 978-1-893361-45-4 **$16.99**

The Secret Book of John: The Gnostic Gospel—Annotated & Explained
Translation & Annotation by Stevan Davies The most significant and influential text of
the ancient Gnostic religion. 5½ x 8½, 208 pp, Quality PB, 978-1-59473-082-5 **$16.99**

JUDAISM

The Divine Feminine in Biblical Wisdom Literature
Selections Annotated & Explained
Translation & Annotation by Rabbi Rami Shapiro; Foreword by Rev. Cynthia Bourgeault, PhD
Uses the Hebrew Bible and Wisdom literature to explain Sophia's way of wisdom
and illustrate Her creative energy. 5½ x 8½, 240 pp, Quality PB, 978-1-59473-109-9 **$16.99**

Ecclesiastes: Annotated & Explained
Translation & Annotation by Rabbi Rami Shapiro; Foreword by Rev. Barbara Cawthorne Crafton
A timeless teaching on living well amid uncertainty and insecurity.
5½ x 8½, 160 pp, Quality PB, 978-1-59473-287-4 **$16.99**

Ethics of the Sages: *Pirke Avot*—Annotated & Explained
Translation & Annotation by Rabbi Rami Shapiro Clarifies the ethical teachings of the
early Rabbis. 5½ x 8½, 192 pp, Quality PB, 978-1-59473-207-2 **$16.99**

Hasidic Tales: Annotated & Explained
Translation & Annotation by Rabbi Rami Shapiro; Foreword by Andrew Harvey
Introduces the legendary tales of the impassioned Hasidic rabbis, presenting them as
stories rather than as parables. 5½ x 8½, 240 pp, Quality PB, 978-1-893361-86-7 **$16.95**

The Hebrew Prophets: Selections Annotated & Explained
Translation & Annotation by Rabbi Rami Shapiro; Foreword by Rabbi Zalman M. Schachter-Shalomi
5½ x 8½, 224 pp, Quality PB, 978-1-59473-037-5 **$16.99**

***Tanya,* the Masterpiece of Hasidic Wisdom:** Selections Annotated &
Explained *Translation & Annotation by Rabbi Rami Shapiro; Foreword by Rabbi Zalman M.
Schachter-Shalomi* Clarifies one of the most powerful and potentially transforma-
tive books of Jewish wisdom. 5½ x 8½, 240 pp, Quality PB, 978-1-59473-275-1 **$16.99**

Zohar: Annotated & Explained *Translation & Annotation by Daniel C. Matt;
Foreword by Andrew Harvey* The canonical text of Jewish mystical tradition.
5½ x 8½, 176 pp, Quality PB, 978-1-893361-51-5 **$15.99**

Sacred Texts—continued

ISLAM

Ghazali on the Principles of Islamic Spirituality
Selections from *Forty Foundations of Religion*—Annotated & Explained
Translation & Annotation by Aaron Spevack, PhD
Makes the core message of this influential spiritual master relevant to anyone seeking a balanced understanding of Islam.
5½ x 8½, 208 pp (est), Quality PB, 978-1-59473-284-3 **$16.99**

The Qur'an and Sayings of Prophet Muhammad
Selections Annotated & Explained
Annotation by Sohaib N. Sultan; Translation by Yusuf Ali, Revised by Sohaib N. Sultan; Foreword by Jane I. Smith
Presents the foundational wisdom of Islam in an easy-to-use format.
5½ x 8½, 256 pp, Quality PB, 978-1-59473-222-5 **$16.99**

Rumi and Islam: Selections from His Stories, Poems, and Discourses—Annotated & Explained *Translation & Annotation by Ibrahim Gamard*
Focuses on Rumi's place within the Sufi tradition of Islam, providing insight into the mystical side of the religion.
5½ x 8½, 240 pp, Quality PB, 978-1-59473-002-3 **$15.99**

EASTERN RELIGIONS

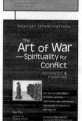

The Art of War—Spirituality for Conflict: Annotated & Explained
by Sun Tzu; Annotation by Thomas Huynh; Translation by Thomas Huynh and the Editors at Sonshi.com; Foreword by Marc Benioff; Preface by Thomas Cleary
Highlights principles that encourage a perceptive and spiritual approach to conflict.
5½ x 8½, 256 pp, Quality PB, 978-1-59473-244-7 **$16.99**

Bhagavad Gita: Annotated & Explained
Translation by Shri Purohit Swami; Annotation by Kendra Crossen Burroughs; Foreword by Andrew Harvey
Presents the classic text's teachings—with no previous knowledge of Hinduism required.
5½ x 8½, 192 pp, Quality PB, 978-1-893361-28-7 **$16.95**

Chuang-tzu: The Tao of Perfect Happiness—Selections Annotated & Explained
Translation & Annotation by Livia Kohn, PhD
Presents Taoism's central message of reverence for the "Way" of the natural world.
5½ x 8½, 240 pp, Quality PB, 978-1-59473-296-6 **$16.99**

Confucius, the *Analects:* The Path of the Sage—Selections Annotated & Explained *Annotation by Rodney L. Taylor, PhD; Translation by James Legge, Revised by Rodney L. Taylor, PhD* Explores the ethical and spiritual meaning behind the Confucian way of learning and self-cultivation.
5½ x 8½, 192 pp, Quality PB, 978-1-59473-306-2 **$16.99**

Dhammapada: Annotated & Explained
Translation by Max Müller, revised by Jack Maguire; Annotation by Jack Maguire; Foreword by Andrew Harvey Contains all of Buddhism's key teachings, plus commentary that explains all the names, terms and references.
5½ x 8½, 160 pp, b/w photos, Quality PB, 978-1-893361-42-3 **$14.95**

Selections from the Gospel of Sri Ramakrishna: Annotated & Explained
Translation by Swami Nikhilananda; Annotation by Kendra Crossen Burroughs; Foreword by Andrew Harvey Introduces the fascinating world of the Indian mystic and the universal appeal of his message.
5½ x 8½, 240 pp, b/w photos, Quality PB, 978-1-893361-46-1 **$16.95**

Tao Te Ching: Annotated & Explained
Translation & Annotation by Derek Lin; Foreword by Lama Surya Das
Introduces an Eastern classic in an accessible, poetic and completely original way.
5½ x 8½, 208 pp, Quality PB, 978-1-59473-204-1 **$16.99**

Sacred Texts—continued

MORMONISM

The Book of Mormon: Selections Annotated & Explained
Annotation by Jana Riess; Foreword by Phyllis Tickle Explores the sacred epic that is cherished by more than twelve million members of the LDS church as the keystone of their faith. 5½ x 8½, 272 pp, Quality PB, 978-1-59473-076-4 **$16.99**

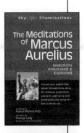

NATIVE AMERICAN

Native American Stories of the Sacred: Annotated & Explained
Retold & Annotated by Evan T. Pritchard These teaching tales contain elegantly simple illustrations of time-honored truths. 5½ x 8½, 272 pp, Quality PB, 978-1-59473-112-9 **$16.99**

STOICISM

The Meditations of Marcus Aurelius: Selections Annotated & Explained *Annotation by Russell McNeil, PhD; Translation by George Long, revised by Russell McNeil, PhD* Ancient Stoic wisdom that speaks vibrantly today about life, business, government and spirit. 5½ x 8½, 288 pp, Quality PB, 978-1-59473-236-2 **$16.99**

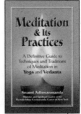

Hinduism / Vedanta

The Four Yogas: A Guide to the Spiritual Paths of Action, Devotion, Meditation and Knowledge *by Swami Adiswarananda*
6 x 9, 320 pp, Quality PB, 978-1-59473-223-2 **$19.99**; HC, 978-1-59473-143-3 **$29.99**

Meditation & Its Practices: A Definitive Guide to Techniques and Traditions of Meditation in Yoga and Vedanta *by Swami Adiswarananda* 6 x 9, 504 pp, Quality PB, 978-1-59473-105-1 **$24.99**

The Spiritual Quest and the Way of Yoga: The Goal, the Journey and the Milestones *by Swami Adiswarananda* 6 x 9, 288 pp, HC, 978-1-59473-113-6 **$29.99**

Sri Ramakrishna, the Face of Silence
by Swami Nikhilananda and Dhan Gopal Mukerji; Edited with an Introduction by Swami Adiswarananda; Foreword by Dhan Gopal Mukerji II 6 x 9, 352 pp, Quality PB, 978-1-59473-233-1 **$21.99**

Sri Sarada Devi, The Holy Mother: Her Teachings and Conversations
Translated with Notes by Swami Nikhilananda; Edited with an Introduction by Swami Adiswarananda
6 x 9, 288 pp, HC, 978-1-59473-070-2 **$29.99**

The Vedanta Way to Peace and Happiness *by Swami Adiswarananda*
6 x 9, 240 pp, Quality PB, 978-1-59473-180-8 **$18.99**; HC, 978-1-59473-034-4 **$29.99**

Vivekananda, World Teacher: His Teachings on the Spiritual Unity of Humankind
Edited and with an Introduction by Swami Adiswarananda
6 x 9, 272 pp, Quality PB, 978-1-59473-210-2 **$21.99**

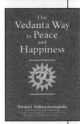

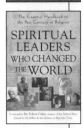

Sikhism

The First Sikh Spiritual Master: Timeless Wisdom from the Life and Teachings of Guru Nanak *by Harish Dhillon* 6 x 9, 192 pp, Quality PB, 978-1-59473-209-6 **$16.99**

Spiritual Biography

Spiritual Leaders Who Changed the World
The Essential Handbook to the Past Century of Religion
Edited by Ira Rifkin and the Editors at SkyLight Paths; Foreword by Dr. Robert Coles
An invaluable reference to the most important spiritual leaders of the past 100 years.
6 x 9, 304 pp, b/w photos, Quality PB, 978-1-59473-241-6 **$18.99**

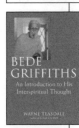

Mahatma Gandhi: His Life and Ideas *by Charles F. Andrews; Foreword by Dr. Arun Gandhi*
Examines the religious ideas and political dynamics that influenced the birth of the peaceful resistance movement. 6 x 9, 336 pp, b/w photos, Quality PB, 978-1-893361-89-8 **$18.95**

Bede Griffiths: An Introduction to His Interspiritual Thought
by Wayne Teasdale The first study of his contemplative experience and thought, exploring the intersection of Hinduism and Christianity.
6 x 9, 288 pp, Quality PB, 978-1-893361-77-5 **$18.95**

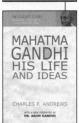

Prayer / Meditation

Sacred Attention: A Spiritual Practice for Finding God in the Moment
by Margaret D. McGee
Framed on the Christian liturgical year, this inspiring guide explores ways to develop a practice of attention as a means of talking—and listening—to God.
6 x 9, 144 pp, Quality PB, 978-1-59473-291-1 **$16.99**

Women of Color Pray: Voices of Strength, Faith, Healing, Hope and Courage
Edited and with Introductions by Christal M. Jackson
Through these prayers, poetry, lyrics, meditations and affirmations, you will share in the strong and undeniable connection women of color share with God.
5 x 7¼, 208 pp, Quality PB, 978-1-59473-077-1 **$15.99**

Secrets of Prayer: A Multifaith Guide to Creating Personal Prayer in Your Life   *by Nancy Corcoran, CSJ*
This compelling, multifaith guidebook offers you companionship and encouragement on the journey to a healthy prayer life. 6 x 9, 160 pp, Quality PB, 978-1-59473-215-7 **$16.99**

Prayers to an Evolutionary God
by William Cleary; Afterword by Diarmuid O'Murchu
Inspired by the spiritual and scientific teachings of Diarmuid O'Murchu and Teilhard de Chardin, reveals that religion and science can be combined to create an expanding view of the universe—an evolutionary faith.
6 x 9, 208 pp, HC, 978-1-59473-006-1 **$21.99**

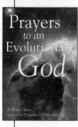

The Art of Public Prayer, 2nd Edition: Not for Clergy Only
by Lawrence A. Hoffman, PhD 6 x 9, 288 pp, Quality PB, 978-1-893361-06-5 **$19.99**

A Heart of Stillness: A Complete Guide to Learning the Art of Meditation
by David A. Cooper 5½ x 8½, 272 pp, Quality PB, 978-1-893361-03-4 **$18.99**

Meditation without Gurus: A Guide to the Heart of Practice
by Clark Strand 5½ x 8½, 192 pp, Quality PB, 978-1-893361-93-5 **$16.95**

Praying with Our Hands: 21 Practices of Embodied Prayer from the World's Spiritual Traditions   *by Jon M. Sweeney; Photos by Jennifer J. Wilson; Foreword by Mother Tessa Bielecki; Afterword by Taitetsu Unno, PhD*
8 x 8, 96 pp, 22 duotone photos, Quality PB, 978-1-893361-16-4 **$16.95**

Three Gates to Meditation Practice: A Personal Journey into Sufism, Buddhism, and Judaism   *by David A. Cooper* 5½ x 8½, 240 pp, Quality PB, 978-1-893361-22-5 **$16.95**

Prayer / M. Basil Pennington, OCSO

Finding Grace at the Center, 3rd Edition: The Beginning of Centering Prayer   *with Thomas Keating, OCSO, and Thomas E. Clarke, SJ; Foreword by Rev. Cynthia Bourgeault, PhD* A practical guide to a simple and beautiful form of meditative prayer. 5 x 7¼, 128 pp, Quality PB, 978-1-59473-182-2 **$12.99**

The Monks of Mount Athos: A Western Monk's Extraordinary Spiritual Journey on Eastern Holy Ground   *Foreword by Archimandrite Dionysios*
Explores the landscape, monastic communities and food of Athos.
6 x 9, 352 pp, Quality PB, 978-1-893361-78-2 **$18.95**

Psalms: A Spiritual Commentary   *Illus. by Phillip Ratner*
Reflections on some of the most beloved passages from the Bible's most widely read book.   6 x 9, 176 pp, 24 full-page b/w illus., Quality PB, 978-1-59473-234-8 **$16.99**

The Song of Songs: A Spiritual Commentary   *Illus. by Phillip Ratner*
Explore the Bible's most challenging mystical text.
6 x 9, 160 pp, 14 full-page b/w illus., Quality PB, 978-1-59473-235-5 **$16.99**
HC, 978-1-59473-004-7 **$19.99**

Women's Interest

Spiritually Healthy Divorce: Navigating Disruption with Insight & Hope
by Carolyne Call
A spiritual map to help you move through the twists and turns of divorce.
6 x 9, 224 pp, Quality PB, 978-1-59473-288-1 **$16.99**

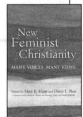

New Feminist Christianity: Many Voices, Many Views
Edited by Mary E. Hunt and Diann L. Neu
Insights from ministers and theologians, activists and leaders, artists and liturgists who are shaping the future. Taken together, their voices offer a starting point for building new models of religious life and worship.
6 x 9, 384 pp, HC, 978-1-59473-285-0 **$24.99**

New Jewish Feminism: Probing the Past, Forging the Future
Edited by Rabbi Elyse Goldstein; Foreword by Anita Diamant
Looks at the growth and accomplishments of Jewish feminism and what they mean for Jewish women today and tomorrow. Features the voices of women from every area of Jewish life, addressing the important issues that concern Jewish women.
6 x 9, 480 pp, Quality PB, 978-1-58023-448-1 **$19.99**; HC, 978-1-58023-359-0 **$24.99***

Bread, Body, Spirit: Finding the Sacred in Food
Edited and with Introductions by Alice Peck
6 x 9, 224 pp, Quality PB, 978-1-59473-242-3 **$19.99**

Dance—The Sacred Art: The Joy of Movement as a Spiritual Practice
by Cynthia Winton-Henry 5½ x 8½, 224 pp, Quality PB, 978-1-59473-268-3 **$16.99**

Daughters of the Desert: Stories of Remarkable Women from Christian, Jewish and Muslim Traditions
by Claire Rudolf Murphy, Meghan Nuttall Sayres, Mary Cronk Farrell, Sarah Conover and Betsy Wharton
5½ x 8½, 192 pp, Illus., Quality PB, 978-1-59473-106-8 **$14.99** Inc. reader's discussion guide

The Divine Feminine in Biblical Wisdom Literature
Selections Annotated & Explained
Translation & Annotation by Rabbi Rami Shapiro; Foreword by Rev. Cynthia Bourgeault, PhD
5½ x 8½, 240 pp, Quality PB, 978-1-59473-109-9 **$16.99**

Divining the Body: Reclaim the Holiness of Your Physical Self
by Jan Phillips 8 x 8, 256 pp, Quality PB, 978-1-59473-080-1 **$16.99**

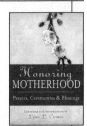

Honoring Motherhood: Prayers, Ceremonies & Blessings
Edited and with Introductions by Lynn L. Caruso 5 x 7¼, 272 pp, HC, 978-1-59473-239-3 **$19.99**

Next to Godliness: Finding the Sacred in Housekeeping
Edited by Alice Peck 6 x 9, 224 pp, Quality PB, 978-1-59473-214-0 **$19.99**

ReVisions: Seeing Torah through a Feminist Lens
by Rabbi Elyse Goldstein 5½ x 8½, 224 pp, Quality PB, 978-1-58023-117-6 **$16.95***

The Triumph of Eve & Other Subversive Bible Tales
by Matt Biers-Ariel 5½ x 8½, 192 pp, Quality PB, 978-1-59473-176-1 **$14.99**

White Fire: A Portrait of Women Spiritual Leaders in America
by Malka Drucker; Photos by Gay Block 7 x 10, 320 pp, b/w photos, HC, 978-1-893361-64-5 **$24.95**

Woman Spirit Awakening in Nature
Growing Into the Fullness of Who You Are
by Nancy Barrett Chickerneo, PhD; Foreword by Eileen Fisher
8 x 8, 224 pp, b/w illus., Quality PB, 978-1-59473-250-8 **$16.99**

Women of Color Pray: Voices of Strength, Faith, Healing, Hope and Courage
Edited and with Introductions by Christal M. Jackson
5 x 7¼, 208 pp, Quality PB, 978-1-59473-077-1 **$15.99**

The Women's Torah Commentary: New Insights from Women Rabbis on the 54
Weekly Torah Portions *Edited by Rabbi Elyse Goldstein*
6 x 9, 496 pp, Quality PB, 978-1-58023-370-5 **$19.99**; HC, 978-1-58023-076-6 **$34.95***

---

* A book from Jewish Lights, SkyLight Paths' sister imprint

Spiritual Practice

Fly Fishing—The Sacred Art: Casting a Fly as a Spiritual Practice
by Rabbi Eric Eisenkramer and Rev. Michael Attas, MD
Illuminates what fly fishing can teach you about reflection, awe and wonder; the benefits of solitude; the blessing of community and the search for the Divine.
5½ x 8½, 192 pp (est), Quality PB, 978-1-59473-299-7 **$16.99**

Lectio Divina—The Sacred Art: Transforming Words & Images into Heart-Centered Prayer *by Christine Valters Paintner, PhD*
Expands the practice of sacred reading beyond scriptural texts and makes it accessible in contemporary life. 5½ x 8½, 240 pp, Quality PB, 978-1-59473-300-0 **$16.99**

Haiku—The Sacred Art: A Spiritual Practice in Three Lines
by Margaret D. McGee 5½ x 8½, 192 pp, Quality PB, 978-1-59473-269-0 **$16.99**

Dance—The Sacred Art: The Joy of Movement as a Spiritual Practice
by Cynthia Winton-Henry 5½ x 8½, 224 pp, Quality PB, 978-1-59473-268-3 **$16.99**

Spiritual Adventures in the Snow: Skiing & Snowboarding as Renewal for Your Soul *by Dr. Marcia McFee and Rev. Karen Foster; Foreword by Paul Arthur*
5½ x 8½, 208 pp, Quality PB, 978-1-59473-270-6 **$16.99**

Divining the Body: Reclaim the Holiness of Your Physical Self *by Jan Phillips*
8 x 8, 256 pp, Quality PB, 978-1-59473-080-1 **$16.99**

Everyday Herbs in Spiritual Life: A Guide to Many Practices
by Michael J. Caduto; Foreword by Rosemary Gladstar
7 x 9, 208 pp, 20+ b/w illus., Quality PB, 978-1-59473-174-7 **$16.99**

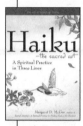

Giving—The Sacred Art: Creating a Lifestyle of Generosity
by Lauren Tyler Wright 5½ x 8½, 208 pp, Quality PB, 978-1-59473-224-9 **$16.99**

Hospitality—The Sacred Art: Discovering the Hidden Spiritual Power of Invitation and Welcome *by Rev. Nanette Sawyer; Foreword by Rev. Dirk Ficca*
5½ x 8½, 208 pp, Quality PB, 978-1-59473-228-7 **$16.99**

Labyrinths from the Outside In: Walking to Spiritual Insight—A Beginner's Guide
by Donna Schaper and Carole Ann Camp
6 x 9, 208 pp, b/w illus. and photos, Quality PB, 978-1-893361-18-8 **$16.95**

Practicing the Sacred Art of Listening: A Guide to Enrich Your Relationships and Kindle Your Spiritual Life *by Kay Lindahl* 8 x 8, 176 pp, Quality PB, 978-1-893361-85-0 **$16.95**

Recovery—The Sacred Art: The Twelve Steps as Spiritual Practice *by Rami Shapiro; Foreword by Joan Borysenko, PhD* 5½ x 8½, 240 pp, Quality PB, 978-1-59473-259-1 **$16.99**

Running—The Sacred Art: Preparing to Practice *by Dr. Warren A. Kay; Foreword by Kristin Armstrong* 5½ x 8½, 160 pp, Quality PB, 978-1-59473-227-0 **$16.99**

The Sacred Art of Chant: Preparing to Practice
by Ana Hernández 5½ x 8½, 192 pp, Quality PB, 978-1-59473-036-8 **$15.99**

The Sacred Art of Fasting: Preparing to Practice
by Thomas Ryan, CSP 5½ x 8½, 192 pp, Quality PB, 978-1-59473-078-8 **$15.99**

The Sacred Art of Forgiveness: Forgiving Ourselves and Others through God's Grace
by Marcia Ford 8 x 8, 176 pp, Quality PB, 978-1-59473-175-4 **$18.99**

The Sacred Art of Listening: Forty Reflections for Cultivating a Spiritual Practice
by Kay Lindahl; Illus. by Amy Schnapper 8 x 8, 160 pp, b/w illus., Quality PB, 978-1-893361-44-7 **$16.99**

The Sacred Art of Lovingkindness: Preparing to Practice
by Rabbi Rami Shapiro; Foreword by Marcia Ford 5½ x 8½, 176 pp, Quality PB, 978-1-59473-151-8 **$16.99**

Sacred Attention: A Spiritual Practice for Finding God in the Moment
by Margaret D. McGee 6 x 9, 144 pp, Quality PB, 978-1-59473-291-1 **$16.99**

Soul Fire: Accessing Your Creativity
by Thomas Ryan, CSP 6 x 9, 160 pp, Quality PB, 978-1-59473-243-0 **$16.99**

Thanking & Blessing—The Sacred Art: Spiritual Vitality through Gratefulness
by Jay Marshall, PhD; Foreword by Philip Gulley 5½ x 8½, 176 pp, Quality PB, 978-1-59473-231-7 **$16.99**

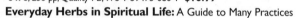

Spirituality

The Heartbeat of God: Finding the Sacred in the Middle of Everything
by Katharine Jefferts Schori; Foreword by Joan Chittister, OSB
Explores our connections to other people, to other nations and with the environment through the lens of faith. 6 x 9, 240 pp, HC, 978-1-59473-292-8 **$21.99**

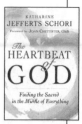

A Dangerous Dozen: Twelve Christians Who Threatened the Status Quo but Taught Us to Live Like Jesus
by the Rev. Canon C. K. Robertson, PhD; Foreword by Archbishop Desmond Tutu
Profiles twelve visionary men and women who challenged society and showed the world a different way of living. 6 x 9, 208 pp, Quality PB, 978-1-59473-298-0 **$16.99**

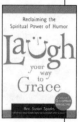

Decision Making & Spiritual Discernment: The Sacred Art of Finding Your Way *by Nancy L. Bieber*
Presents three essential aspects of Spirit-led decision making: willingness, attentiveness and responsiveness. 5½ x 8½, 208 pp, Quality PB, 978-1-59473-289-8 **$16.99**

Laugh Your Way to Grace: Reclaiming the Spiritual Power of Humor
by Rev. Susan Sparks A powerful, humorous case for laughter as a spiritual, healing path. 6 x 9, 176 pp, Quality PB, 978-1-59473-280-5 **$16.99**

Living into Hope: A Call to Spiritual Action for Such a Time as This
by Rev. Dr. Joan Brown Campbell; Foreword by Karen Armstrong
A visionary minister speaks out on the pressing issues that face us today, offering inspiration and challenge. 6 x 9, 208 pp, HC, 978-1-59473-283-6 **$21.99**

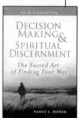

Claiming Earth as Common Ground: The Ecological Crisis through the Lens of Faith
by Andrea Cohen-Kiener; Foreword by Rev. Sally Bingham
6 x 9, 192 pp, Quality PB, 978-1-59473-261-4 **$16.99**

Bread, Body, Spirit: Finding the Sacred in Food
Edited and with Introductions by Alice Peck 6 x 9, 224 pp, Quality PB, 978-1-59473-242-3 **$19.99**

Creating a Spiritual Retirement: A Guide to the Unseen Possibilities in Our Lives
by Molly Srode 6 x 9, 208 pp, b/w photos, Quality PB, 978-1-59473-050-4 **$14.99**

Creative Aging: Rethinking Retirement and Non-Retirement in a Changing World
by Marjory Zoet Bankson 6 x 9, 160 pp, Quality PB, 978-1-59473-281-2 **$16.99**

Keeping Spiritual Balance as We Grow Older: More than 65 Creative Ways to Use Purpose, Prayer, and the Power of Spirit to Build a Meaningful Retirement
by Molly and Bernie Srode 8 x 8, 224 pp, Quality PB, 978-1-59473-042-9 **$16.99**

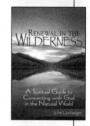

Hearing the Call across Traditions: Readings on Faith and Service
Edited by Adam Davis; Foreword by Eboo Patel
6 x 9, 352 pp, Quality PB, 978-1-59473-303-1 **$18.99**; HC, 978-1-59473-264-5 **$29.99**

Honoring Motherhood: Prayers, Ceremonies & Blessings
Edited and with Introductions by Lynn L. Caruso 5 x 7¼, 272 pp, HC, 978-1-59473-239-3 **$19.99**

Journeys of Simplicity: Traveling Light with Thomas Merton, Bashō, Edward Abbey, Annie Dillard & Others *by Philip Harnden*
5 x 7¼, 144 pp, Quality PB, 978-1-59473-181-5 **$12.99**; 128 pp, HC, 978-1-893361-76-8 **$16.95**

The Losses of Our Lives: The Sacred Gifts of Renewal in Everyday Loss
by Dr. Nancy Copeland-Payton 6 x 9, 192 pp, HC, 978-1-59473-271-3 **$19.99**

Renewal in the Wilderness: A Spiritual Guide to Connecting with God in the Natural World *by John Lionberger*
6 x 9, 176 pp, b/w photos, Quality PB, 978-1-59473-219-5 **$16.99**

Soul Fire: Accessing Your Creativity
by Thomas Ryan, CSP 6 x 9, 160 pp, Quality PB, 978-1-59473-243-0 **$16.99**

A Spirituality for Brokenness: Discovering Your Deepest Self in Difficult Times
by Terry Taylor 6 x 9, 176 pp, Quality PB, 978-1-59473-229-4 **$16.99**

A Walk with Four Spiritual Guides: Krishna, Buddha, Jesus, and Ramakrishna
by Andrew Harvey 5½ x 8½, 192 pp, b/w photos & illus., Quality PB, 978-1-59473-138-9 **$15.99**

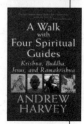

The Workplace and Spirituality: New Perspectives on Research and Practice
Edited by Dr. Joan Marques, Dr. Satinder Dhiman and Dr. Richard King
6 x 9, 256 pp, HC, 978-1-59473-260-7 **$29.99**

Bible Stories / Folktales

Abraham's Bind & Other Bible Tales of Trickery, Folly, Mercy and Love by Michael J. Caduto

New retellings of episodes in the lives of familiar biblical characters explore relevant life lessons.   6 x 9, 224 pp, HC, 978-1-59473-186-0 **$19.99**

Daughters of the Desert: Stories of Remarkable Women from Christian, Jewish and Muslim Traditions by Claire Rudolf Murphy,
Meghan Nuttall Sayres, Mary Cronk Farrell, Sarah Conover and Betsy Wharton

Breathes new life into the old tales of our female ancestors in faith. Uses traditional scriptural passages as starting points, then with vivid detail fills in historical context and place. Chapters reveal the voices of Sarah, Hagar, Huldah, Esther, Salome, Mary Magdalene, Lydia, Khadija, Fatima and many more. Historical fiction ideal for readers of all ages.

5½ x 8½, 192 pp, Quality PB, 978-1-59473-106-8 **$14.99**   Inc. reader's discussion guide
HC, 978-1-893361-72-0 **$19.95**

The Triumph of Eve & Other Subversive Bible Tales
by Matt Biers-Ariel

These engaging retellings of familiar Bible stories are witty, often hilarious and always profound. They invite you to grapple with questions and issues that are often hidden in the original texts.

5½ x 8½, 192 pp, Quality PB, 978-1-59473-176-1 **$14.99**

Also available: **The Triumph of Eve Teacher's Guide**
8½ x 11, 44 pp, PB, 978-1-59473-152-5 **$8.99**

Wisdom in the Telling
Finding Inspiration and Grace in Traditional Folktales and Myths Retold
by Lorraine Hartin-Gelardi
6 x 9, 192 pp, HC, 978-1-59473-185-3 **$19.99**

Religious Etiquette / Reference

How to Be a Perfect Stranger, 5th Edition: The Essential Religious Etiquette Handbook Edited by Stuart M. Matlins and Arthur J. Magida

The indispensable guidebook to help the well-meaning guest when visiting other people's religious ceremonies. A straightforward guide to the rituals and celebrations of the major religions and denominations in the United States and Canada from the perspective of an interested guest of any other faith, based on information obtained from authorities of each religion. Belongs in every living room, library and office. Covers:

African American Methodist Churches • Assemblies of God • Bahá'í Faith • Baptist • Buddhist • Christian Church (Disciples of Christ) • Christian Science (Church of Christ, Scientist) • Churches of Christ • Episcopalian and Anglican • Hindu • Islam • Jehovah's Witnesses • Jewish • Lutheran • Mennonite/Amish • Methodist • Mormon (Church of Jesus Christ of Latter-day Saints) • Native American/First Nations • Orthodox Churches • Pentecostal Church of God • Presbyterian • Quaker (Religious Society of Friends) • Reformed Church in America/Canada • Roman Catholic • Seventh-day Adventist • Sikh • Unitarian Universalist • United Church of Canada • United Church of Christ

"The things Miss Manners forgot to tell us about religion."

—*Los Angeles Times*

"Finally, for those inclined to undertake their own spiritual journeys ... tells visitors what to expect."   —*New York Times*

6 x 9, 432 pp, Quality PB, 978-1-59473-294-2 **$19.99**

The Perfect Stranger's Guide to Funerals and Grieving Practices: A Guide to Etiquette in Other People's Religious Ceremonies Edited by Stuart M. Matlins
6 x 9, 240 pp, Quality PB, 978-1-893361-20-1 **$16.95**

The Perfect Stranger's Guide to Wedding Ceremonies: A Guide to Etiquette in Other People's Religious Ceremonies Edited by Stuart M. Matlins
6 x 9, 208 pp, Quality PB, 978-1-893361-19-5 **$16.95**

Judaism / Christianity / Islam / Interfaith

Christians & Jews—Faith to Faith: Tragic History, Promising Present, Fragile Future *by Rabbi James Rudin*
A probing examination of Christian-Jewish relations that looks at the major issues facing both faith communities. 6 x 9, 288 pp, HC, 978-1-58023-432-0 **$24.99***

Getting to the Heart of Interfaith
The Eye-Opening, Hope-Filled Friendship of a Pastor, a Rabbi and a Sheikh
by Pastor Don Mackenzie, Rabbi Ted Falcon and Imam Jamal Rahman
Offers many insights and encouragements for individuals and groups who want to tap into the promise of interfaith dialogue. 6 x 9, 192 pp, Quality PB, 978-1-59473-263-8 **$16.99**

Hearing the Call across Traditions: Readings on Faith and Service
Edited by Adam Davis; Foreword by Eboo Patel
Explores the connections between faith, service and social justice through the prose, verse and sacred texts of the world's great faith traditions.
6 x 9, 352 pp, Quality PB, 978-1-59473-303-1 **$18.99**; HC, 978-1-59473-264-5 **$29.99**

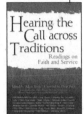

How to Do Good & Avoid Evil: A Global Ethic from the Sources of Judaism
by Hans Küng and Rabbi Walter Homolka; Translated by Rev. Dr. John Bowden
6 x 9, 224 pp, HC, 978-1-59473-255-3 **$19.99**

Blessed Relief: What Christians Can Learn from Buddhists about Suffering
by Gordon Peerman 6 x 9, 208 pp, Quality PB, 978-1-59473-252-2 **$16.99**

The Changing Christian World: A Brief Introduction for Jews
by Rabbi Leonard A. Schoolman 5½ x 8½, 176 pp, Quality PB, 978-1-58023-344-6 **$16.99***

Christians & Jews in Dialogue: Learning in the Presence of the Other *by Mary C. Boys and Sara S. Lee; Foreword by Dorothy C. Bass* 6 x 9, 240 pp, Quality PB, 978-1-59473-254-6 **$18.99**

Disaster Spiritual Care: Practical Clergy Responses to Community, Regional and National Tragedy *Edited by Rabbi Stephen B. Roberts, BCJC, and Rev. Willard W. C. Ashley, Sr., DMin, DH*
6 x 9, 384 pp, HC, 978-1-59473-240-9 **$40.00**

InterActive Faith: The Essential Interreligious Community-Building Handbook
Edited by Rev. Bud Heckman with Rori Picker Neiss; Foreword by Rev. Dirk Ficca
6 x 9, 304 pp, Quality PB, 978-1-59473-273-7 **$16.99**; HC, 978-1-59473-237-9 **$29.99**

The Jewish Approach to God: A Brief Introduction for Christians
by Rabbi Neil Gillman, PhD 5½ x 8½, 192 pp, Quality PB, 978-1-58023-190-9 **$16.95***

The Jewish Approach to Repairing the World (*Tikkun Olam*): A Brief Introduction for Christians *by Rabbi Elliot N. Dorff, PhD, with Rev. Cory Willson*
5½ x 8½, 256 pp, Quality PB, 978-1-58023-349-1 **$16.99***

The Jewish Connection to Israel, the Promised Land: A Brief Introduction for Christians *by Rabbi Eugene Korn, PhD* 5½ x 8½, 192 pp, Quality PB, 978-1-58023-318-7 **$14.99***

Jewish Holidays: A Brief Introduction for Christians *by Rabbi Kerry M. Olitzky and Rabbi Daniel Judson* 5½ x 8½, 176 pp, Quality PB, 978-1-58023-302-6 **$16.99***

Jewish Ritual: A Brief Introduction for Christians
by Rabbi Kerry M. Olitzky and Rabbi Daniel Judson 5½ x 8½, 144 pp, Quality PB, 978-1-58023-210-4 **$14.99***

Jewish Spirituality: A Brief Introduction for Christians *by Rabbi Lawrence Kushner*
5½ x 8½, 112 pp, Quality PB, 978-1-58023-150-3 **$12.95***

A Jewish Understanding of the New Testament *by Rabbi Samuel Sandmel;*
New preface by Rabbi David Sandmel 5½ x 8½, 368 pp, Quality PB, 978-1-59473-048-1 **$19.99***

Modern Jews Engage the New Testament: Enhancing Jewish Well-Being in a Christian Environment *by Rabbi Michael J. Cook, PhD* 6 x 9, 416 pp, HC, 978-1-58023-313-2 **$29.99***

Talking about God: Exploring the Meaning of Religious Life with Kierkegaard, Buber, Tillich and Heschel *by Daniel F. Polish, PhD* 6 x 9, 160 pp, Quality PB, 978-1-59473-272-0 **$16.99**

We Jews and Jesus: Exploring Theological Differences for Mutual Understanding
by Rabbi Samuel Sandmel; New preface by Rabbi David Sandmel
6 x 9, 192 pp, Quality PB, 978-1-59473-208-9 **$16.99**

Who Are the *Real* Chosen People? The Meaning of Chosenness in Judaism, Christianity and Islam *by Reuven Firestone, PhD*
6 x 9, 176 pp, Quality PB, 978-1-59473-290-4 **$16.99**; HC, 978-1-59473-248-5 **$21.99**

* A book from Jewish Lights, SkyLight Paths' sister imprint

About SKYLIGHT PATHS Publishing

SkyLight Paths Publishing is creating a place where people of different spiritual traditions come together for challenge and inspiration, a place where we can help each other understand the mystery that lies at the heart of our existence.

Through spirituality, our religious beliefs are increasingly becoming a part of our lives—rather than *apart* from our lives. While many of us may be more interested than ever in spiritual growth, we may be less firmly planted in traditional religion. Yet, we do want to deepen our relationship to the sacred, to learn from our own as well as from other faith traditions, and to practice in new ways.

SkyLight Paths sees both believers and seekers as a community that increasingly transcends traditional boundaries of religion and denomination—people wanting to learn from each other, *walking together, finding the way.*

For your information and convenience, at the back of this book we have provided a list of other SkyLight Paths books you might find interesting and useful. They cover the following subjects:

Buddhism / Zen	Global Spiritual	Monasticism
Catholicism	Perspectives	Mysticism
Children's Books	Gnosticism	Poetry
Christianity	Hinduism /	Prayer
Comparative	Vedanta	Religious Etiquette
Religion	Inspiration	Retirement
Current Events	Islam / Sufism	Spiritual Biography
Earth-Based	Judaism	Spiritual Direction
Spirituality	Kabbalah	Spirituality
Enneagram	Meditation	Women's Interest
	Midrash Fiction	Worship

Or phone, fax, mail or e-mail to: SKYLIGHT PATHS Publishing
Sunset Farm Offices, Route 4 • P.O. Box 237 • Woodstock, Vermont 05091
Tel: (802) 457-4000 • Fax: (802) 457-4004 • www.skylightpaths.com
Credit card orders: (800) 962-4544 (8:30AM–5:30PM ET Monday–Friday)
Generous discounts on quantity orders. SATISFACTION GUARANTEED. Prices subject to change.